12/06

746. 46

W9-CQB-416

CLASSIC QUILTS

Susan Harris

YUBA COUNTY LIBRARY
MARYSVILLE, CA

A J.B. Fairfax Press Publication

EDITORIAL
MANAGING EDITOR
Judy Poulos
EDITORIAL ASSISTANT
Ella Martin
EDITORIAL COORDINATOR
Margaret Kelly

PHOTOGRAPHY
Andrew Payne
STYLING
Kathy Tripp

PRODUCTION AND DESIGN
MANAGER
Anna Maguire
PRODUCTION COORDINATION
Meredith Johnston
PRODUCTION COORDINATOR
Sophie Potter
DESIGN MANAGER
Drew Buckmaster
LAYOUT
Lulu Dougherty
CONCEPT DESIGN
Jenny Pace

PUBLISHED BY J.B. Fairfax Press Pty Limited
80-82 McLachlan Ave
Rushcutters Bay
Australia 2011
A.C.N. 003 738 430

WEB ADDRESS: http://www.jbfp.com.au

FORMATTED BY J.B. Fairfax Press Pty Limited

PRINTED BY Toppan Printing Co. Singapore
© J.B. Fairfax Press Pty Limited 1997

This book is copyright. The written instructions, designs,
projects and patterns are intended for the personal, non-
commercial use of the purchaser. No part may be reproduced
by any process without the written permission of the publisher.
Enquiries should be made in writing
to the publisher.

The information in this book is provided in good faith
with no guarantee implied.

JBFP 479

CLASSIC QUILTS
ISBN 1 86343 305 8

YUBA COUNTY LIBRARY
MARYSVILLE, CA

Contents

Introduction

I wrote this book because I not only enjoy making, collecting, reading about, and looking at traditional quilts, but I also love to help other people to make them as well. My fascination for traditional quilts began with the fact that they were originally made for utilitarian purposes, but have evolved into superb examples of individual creativity. Using imaginative composition, these early patchworkers based all their quilts on traditional designs and patterns. The decoration ranged from minimal to inspirational.

While it is generally accepted that modern quilting had its origins in Europe, it was the American immigrant, settling a New World, who was primarily responsible for the development of patchwork and quilting as we know it today. The image of pioneer women with little resources and huge responsibilities making these intensely personal pieces of art stays with me while I quilt. Even the names given to the traditional blocks, such as Turkey Tracks, Log Cabin, Wild Goose Chase, Court House Steps, Windmills and even the sadly named Coffin, evoke the frontier life and the events that shaped these women's lives.

These women were taught needlework by their mothers – no classes or a helpful patchwork shop for them. Designs were passed from mother to daughter, friend to friend. Among the Amish, quilt patterns passed from one group to another, often subtly changed, but remaining essentially the same. Bear's Paw of the west became Duck's Foot in the Mud in the southern states, reflecting changed circumstances, but not radically changing the design. Each quiltmaker could use a popular pattern in a new way, change the borders, add lattice strips or set the blocks on point. In fact, it is often difficult to recognise that two very different quilts are using the same block.

The other aspect of traditional quilts that I like is that the pieced quilts enabled the use of precious scraps of fabric; fabric was so hard to come by in those days, but economic necessity often produced exquisite quilts made of scraps. Keepsake quilts used fabrics from family celebrations (or tragedies), so that Grandma's wedding dress could be pointed out in the quilt adorning one of the family beds. Recycling in the nicest form!

The quilts produced in this fashion were a tribute to the quilter's patience and her frugality. Given the circumstances, the quiltmaker used what they had at hand, combined with an eye for colour and design. For many, the only beauty in their lives was created through their needlework.

The quilts that they produced were intended for use, even those 'put away for best'. Often they were given as gifts to newlyweds, to young men on their coming of age, and were almost always part of a young woman's dowry. The quiltmakers probably had no idea that future generations would cherish their quilts, study their needlework, collect their utilitarian possessions and marvel at their artistry.

Museums today catalogue the work of these quiltmakers, place value on the fabrics, detect the owner's social standing and even count the stitches per inch to determine the quality of workmanship. I am sure these quiltmakers, if they had understood the fate of their work, would have firstly been astonished, then probably embarrassed.

Made for family or close friends, these quilts reflected the love or admiration the maker had for the recipient. A 'Double Wedding Ring' celebrated marriage, an 'Album' quilt took best wishes into a new life, and 'Jacob's Ladder', 'Joseph's Coat', 'Crown of Thorns' and 'Star of Bethlehem' reflected the religious elements of their lives.

Quilts generally, and traditional quilts in particular, have the capacity to bring to life the history of the maker like no other art form. The life and times, the style and the artistry are all embodied in the quilts we love so much today.

With all the resources that are available to us today — the magnificent fabrics, the workshops, the sewing machines and other tools — we are far better equipped to produce quilts that will last for generations and be the heirlooms of the future. We too have the love for family and friends, we have the occasions, we have the need of useful and beautiful quilts to decorate our homes. Often, all that we lack is the recognition of our own talent, and the determination to succeed.

My greatest concern is that people who are not experienced needleworkers are discouraged by their lack of confidence. So many times I have heard comments such as 'I could never do that' or 'I can't sew that well'. Every person who has the desire to pick up a needle and sew is more than capable of producing a quilt that is a wonderful expression of their talent. If at first you don't succeed . . .

Take the opportunity to make something that will give you pleasure while you work on it and will continue to bring pleasure while it is used. Every quilt that you make will be cherished by the recipient. Love is a gift that is truly homemade.

I hope that this book gives you the technique, the inspiration, and the enthusiasm to make a classic quilt.

Susan

About the Author

My lifelong interest in sewing expanded into patchwork and quilting when my neighbour came home from a craft class and showed me her hexagon project. I was hooked! Hexagons appeared on cushions, my daughters' dresses, pillowcases and pincushions.

Then I bought an American needlecraft magazine, featuring a wonderful Anne Oliver quilt. The instructions caused more confusion than satisfaction – I may even finish the quilt one day!

Next, came a move to Roleystone, Western Australia, a notice at the YWCA and attendance at my first patchwork class and everything fell into place. Over two hundred quilts (finished!) have resulted from that class.

The joy quilting has given me extended to being able to fulfil one of my ambitions and open a patchwork shop, Hearts and Hands, in Bullaburra, New South Wales. This was the ultimate combination of work and play, allowing me to share my love of quilting through teaching others and meeting so many dedicated and enthusiastic fellow quilters.

I get great pleasure in the acclaim won by many of my students, several of whom had not made a quilt until joining one of my classes, and also being awarded prizes for my quilts over the years, and having my work featured in several publications.

My love for traditional quilts continues to grow. I am always looking for quicker ways to produce quilts, so that I will have the time necessary to make the many quilts on my list.

TRUNK FROM SENTIMENTAL JOURNEY ANTIQUES, WOOLLAHRA NSW

General Instructions

All of the quilts featured in this book use quick cutting and piecing techniques. The 'Scrap Sunburst' quilt on page 70 also uses templates.

MEASUREMENTS

Measurements for all the quilts are given in metric and imperial measurements. These measurements are not exact conversions. Make sure that you choose and continue to use one or the other. Do not change during the project or problems will occur!

EQUIPMENT

■ Rotary cutter, cutting mat, large and small quilter's rulers, and a large set square will enable you to cut your fabrics easily and accurately. If you are purchasing a rotary cutter for the first time, it is wise to ask your supplier for a hands-on demonstration.

■ A sewing machine in good working order is essential. Start each project with a new needle in your machine. This will help save wear and tear on your machine.

■ Long pins, a 'quick unpick' and good-quality scissors are other essentials.

■ An iron and ironing board should be set up near your sewing machine.

FABRICS

One hundred per cent cotton fabrics are more suitable for patchwork than polyester or blend fabrics. Wash all fabrics before use to ensure they will not bleed in a finished quilt. For dark fabrics, continue washing until the rinse water is clear. Press the fabrics with a dry iron while they are still slightly damp.

With the enormous range of fabric available today, it can be quite difficult to make a choice. Start with one colour that appeals to you, then look for lighter and darker fabrics in similar colours, then choose a contrast. Tiny checks, large and small florals, and geometric prints are always useful. Patchwork shop owners are always a great help. Working with fabrics constantly, they can put together several colours quickly. Don't be afraid to ask for advice, but remember the final choice is yours. By experimenting and being a bit daring, you will have an interesting and unique quilt.

For this book, I have used my favourite fabric colours, reminiscent of traditional quilts. However, the quilts featured here could easily be made in any number of colour combinations, as you can see in the colour variations I have included.

CUTTING

All fabric will stretch to a greater or lesser degree. The bias (or diagonal) of the fabric stretches the most (Fig. 1). The lengthwise grain will stretch the least.

All the fabric in this book is cut across the width, unless specified otherwise. It is important to cut as close to the grain as is possible.

Start by folding the fabric selvage to selvage. Move the top layer until you are satisfied that the fold is sitting flat and the selvages are aligned. You may now find that the crosswise edges are not aligned. To cut straight strips, you will need to tidy up this uneven edge. To do this, align a small ruler or set square with the fold of the fabric and place the larger ruler down the side of the small ruler or set square (Fig. 2). Remove the set square and cut off the uneven edge with the rotary cutter. Work from the opposite end if you are left-handed. Always cut away from you, moving your hand up the ruler as you cut. Remember to replace the safety catch of the rotary cutter until you are ready to use it again.

To cut multiple squares or rectangles, cut strips the desired width plus the seam allowance. Align the top of the ruler with the edge of the fabric and cut squares the width of the strip and rectangles the required length.

Triangles

In traditional quilts, triangles are often used as an essential part of the design. Although all the measurements have been given in the instructions, a working knowledge of why these measurements are used will help you to make quilts in the future.

Some designs in this book require squares made from two triangles. These units are called half-square triangles, and are formed when a square is cut in half, diagonally. To allow for the seam allowance,

the square must be cut 2.5 cm ($7/8$ in) larger than the required finished size.

The formulae for cutting quarter-square triangles is the finished size plus 3.5 cm ($1 1/4$ in).

The formulae for side triangles for blocks on point is: block size times one and a half. For example: a 16 cm block times one and a half means a 24 cm square. A $6 1/2$ in block times one and a half means a $9 3/4$ in square. Cut a square the required size, and cut it twice, diagonally, to yield four side triangles.

SEWING

When sewing rows, press the seams in opposite directions (Fig. 3). The seams will be nicely matched and will sit flat when you join the rows.

When making multiple units, sew the pieces together without cutting the threads between them until all the units are sewn (Fig. 4). Press the seams to the dark side, if different shades of fabric are used.

To sew quarter-square triangles to squares, mark the halfway point along one

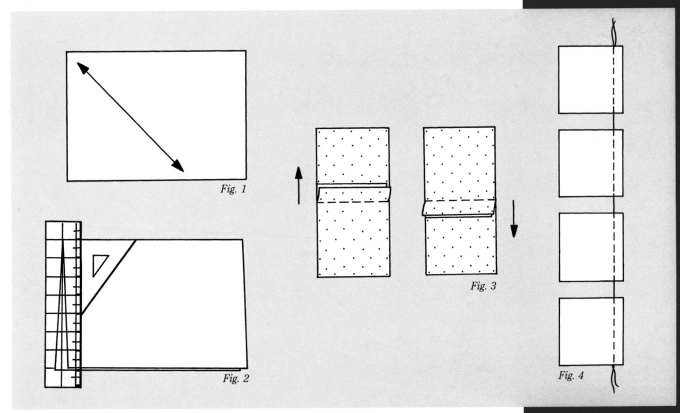

Fig. 1

Fig. 2

Fig. 3

Fig. 4

side of the square and the halfway point of the long side of the triangle. Pin and sew from the inside corner to the inside corner.

Sewing triangles to triangles

When sewing a small triangle to a large triangle (as in 'Turkey Tracks' page 36 or 'Wild Goose Chase' on page 23) place the smaller triangle over the larger triangle and, with the right sides together, sew from the top to the outer corner. The top triangle will appear too big (Fig. 5). Open out the triangles and repeat on the other side (Fig. 6). Trim off the 'ears' (Fig. 7).

Seam allowances

All seams in piecing are 7.5 mm (^{1}/4 in). It is necessary to find the accurate measurement for this when using your machine. Measure with your ruler from the needle to the edge of the presser foot. If this measurement is not the required width, move your needle, if the machine allows. Otherwise, place a small piece of masking tape on the throat plate to indicate the correct distance.

Cut three short 4.5 cm (1^1/2 in) wide strips of waste fabric. Sew the three strips together and press the seams towards the outer strips. The centre strip should measure 3 cm (1 in). If not, adjust the needle or move the tape, until you have the correct measurement.

Sewing strips

Some machines feed fabric layers through unevenly, and this will cause strips to become wavy. When sewing long strips together, pin them at regular intervals to help keep them even. After sewing the seams, and with the darker fabric on top, press the strips, still closed, along the stitching line. Lift the darker fabric up, open it out and press again. The seam will lie towards the darker side.

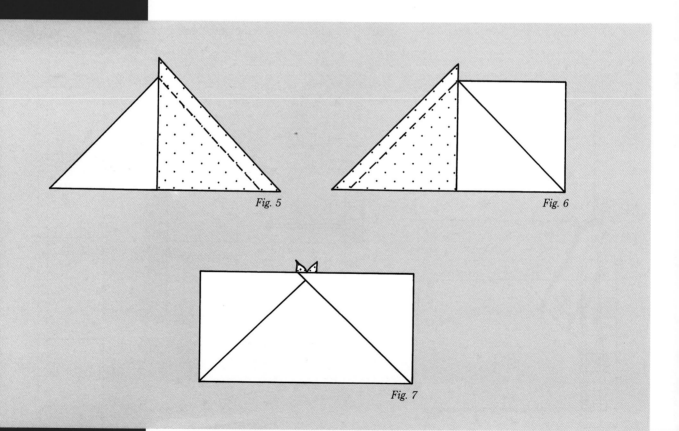

Fig. 5

Fig. 6

Fig. 7

BORDERS

Straight borders

Where possible, the borders on the quilts in this book have been cut lengthwise to avoid joins. However, this method was not practical for all the quilts. Where there are joined borders, the number of strips are specified in the cutting instructions. Sew these strips together with diagonal seams, using a closely matching sewing thread and a smaller-than-usual stitch. Press the seams open. Diagonal seams will be far less noticeable in the border than straight seams. When all the strips are joined together, cut the required lengths from this long strip.

To cut the correct lengths for straight borders, measure the length of the pressed quilt top down the centre, then measure the length at both sides. All three measurements should be the same. Should there be a difference between them, remedy the problem before attaching the border.

To attach straight borders, match the halfway point of the border and of the quilt top and pin them together. Pin the ends of the border and of the quilt top together. Place a number of pins in between these for added accuracy, then sew on the border.

Mitred borders

Measure across and down the centre of the quilt top. Cut the borders to this length plus twice the width of the border. For example, if the borders are cut 10.5 cm (4 in) wide, add 21 cm (8 in) to the required length.

Match the halfway point of the border to the halfway point of the quilt and pin them together. Sew on the borders, beginning and ending the seam 7.5 mm (^{1}/4 in) from each corner (Fig. 8).

Turn the quilt to the right side on the ironing board and, working on one corner at a time, turn under the overlapping ends at an angle of 45 degrees. Use your ruler or set square as a guide. Press this angle. This crease is your sewing line. Sew along the crease line, but do not sew over any other seams (Fig. 9). Trim the seam.

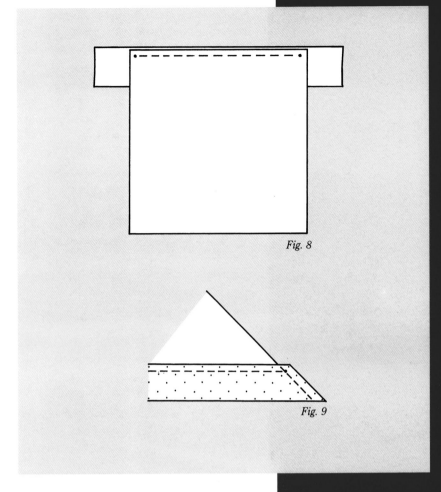

Fig. 8

Fig. 9

BACKING AND BASTING

It is important to choose a backing fabric that is not darker than the front of your quilt to avoid shadowing. Choose a lightweight cotton that is not too tightly woven as this will be easier to quilt.

The backing should be at least 5 cm (2 in) bigger all the way around than the quilt.

For basting, lay the backing fabric out on a flat surface, wrong side up. A large table, such as a ping-pong table, is ideal; however, if one is not available, use the floor. Tape the opposite sides of the backing down to the work surface to keep it taut. Centre the wadding on the backing and smooth out any wrinkles. Centre the quilt top on the wadding, and pin all three layers together with safety pins to hold them together while you are basting. Trim the wadding to within 2 cm (1 in) of the quilt top.

Using a long needle and light-coloured thread, baste all three layers together with a running stitch. Start in the middle and work out towards the sides and the corners of the quilt, forming a grid no larger than 12.5 cm (5 in) (Fig. 10).

Remove the pins and the tape. Fold the edges of the backing over the raw edges of the quilt top and the wadding, and baste them to the front. This will protect the edges of your quilt from snagging or fraying.

QUILTING AND TYING

Many of the quilts in this book have been hand-quilted in traditional designs, using purchased stencils. This is a very convenient way to hand-quilt a design, and there is a great variety of stencils available.

Hand-quilting

To begin hand-quilting, you will need quilting needles, a quilting frame, good-quality quilting thread, small scissors, thimble, quilting stencils and a marking pen. If you are using a washable blue marking pen, always test it on a small piece of fabric used in the quilt, to make sure it is removable.

I always use a circular wooden frame for centre quilting, and a plastic clip frame for border quilting.

Quilting needles come in a wide variety of sizes, all relative to the size of the quilting stitches to be made. Select a needle that suits your style of quilting and is comfortable for you to use for long periods.

Place your frame in the centre of the quilt. Make sure there are no puckers on the front or back. Ensure that the quilt is taut, but still comfortable to work with, and easily quilted. Make a small knot in one end of a quilting thread which is no longer than 50 cm (20 in). Put the needle into the top layer of the quilt, 1–2 cm (3/4 in) away from where you want to start. Come up where you wish your quilting to start and pull the knot gently until it pops through the top layer into the wadding, then take one small back stitch along the line.

Place your thimble on your second finger and take one stitch through all the layers, feeling underneath with your other hand. By just using the tip of the needle to quilt, your stitches will be small. The further you push the needle through, the larger the resulting stitch will be.

Many of my students have developed confidence in this technique by making a mock block of soft fabrics and thin wadding and practising on it. Once you are proficient, you can make multiple quilting stitches on the needle.

If you are quilting right to the edge of the quilt, it is a good idea to baste some calico strips to the borders before basting the quilt. This will allow the very edge of your quilt to fit into the frame.

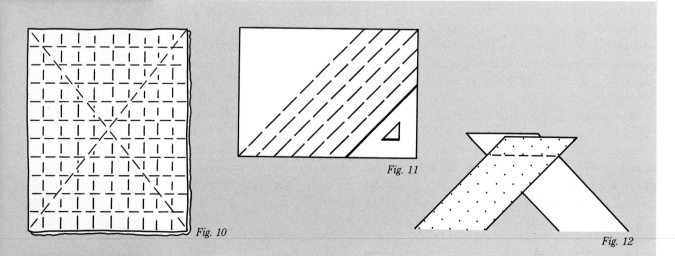

Fig. 10

Fig. 11

Fig. 12

Machine-quilting

If you are doing the machine-quilting yourself, you must mark the design on the quilt top, before assembling and pinning the layers together. Once this is done, prepare the quilt as for hand-quilting, but do not baste it with thread. Use small steel safety pins instead. These can be purchased in large quantities at your local patchwork shop. Start to pin in the centre of the quilt and work out towards the edges, placing the pins no further than 10 cm (4 in) apart.

If you have not machine-quilted before, it is a good idea to do a practice piece first. Make a small (approximately 50 cm (20 in) square) mock quilt with two pieces of plain fabric and a piece of the same wadding that you intend to use for your quilt. Draw several lines approximately 2.5 cm (1 in) apart, down the length of the piece. To begin, put the needle down on one of the lines, just a little in front of where you wish to start. Adjust the stitch length so it is quite small and reverse-stitch back to your starting point. Now stitch forward over the stitches you have just made. Stop and return the stitch length to normal. Place your hands flat on either side of the needle and sew almost to the end of the line. Reduce the stitch length again and stitch to the end, then reverse over the stitches you have just made. Look closely at the stitching down the line. If you wish, adjust the stitch length and practise on another line. When you are happy with a line of stitching, make a note of the stitch length and tension for future reference.

Now, draw some circles and wavy lines on your mock quilt and practise on these in the same way as for the straight lines. Keep practising until you feel confident enough to start on the quilt proper.

For a large quilt, work on a quarter at a time; for a small quilt, start in the middle and work outwards.

A walking foot attachment is available for most sewing machines. It helps to feed the layers of fabric through evenly and helps to prevent puckering. A walking foot is helpful, but not essential. Try quilting on your mock quilt to see if you need one. If you do decide to purchase the attachment, have it fitted at a sewing machine centre to ensure that you get the correct size for your sewing machine. A dual-feed machine does not need a walking foot.

If you are going to use the services of a professional machine-quilter, check their requirements before you assemble your quilt. Some may want you to pin or baste, others prefer to do it themselves.

Tying

You will need to baste your quilt as for hand-quilting. Use crochet thread, Perle cotton or candlewicking thread and a larger-than-usual quilting hoop.

Select the point where you wish to tie and, using a long doubled thread and a darning needle, push the needle down through all layers from the top. If you prefer the ties to be on the underside of the quilt, begin the tie from the underside. Bring the needle up again, close to where it was inserted. Tie a reef knot (left over right, right over left), then trim the threads to the required length. I usually leave them at approximately 2.5 cm (1 in). Continue tying and cutting until all the ties are done. Ties should be no more than 12.5 cm (5 in) apart.

BINDING

The width of the binding can vary to suit the quilt: 50 cm (20 in) of full-width fabric will yield 10 m (11 yd) of 5.5 cm (2¼ in) wide binding; 60 cm (24 in) of full-width fabric will yield 11.5 m (12½ yd) of 5.5 cm (2¼ in) wide binding; and a 60 cm (24 in) square of fabric will yield 6 m (6½ yd) of 5.5 cm (2¼ in) wide bias binding.

To cut bias binding, place a 45 degree angle of your ruler or set square down the side of the fabric and make the first diagonal cut. Continue cutting at 5.5 cm (2¼ in) intervals until you have the desired length (Fig. 11). Join strips together with diagonal seams to make one long strip (Fig 12).

Fold the binding strip in half, lengthwise, for a double layer. Press flat.

Trim the wadding and backing to the size of the quilt top.

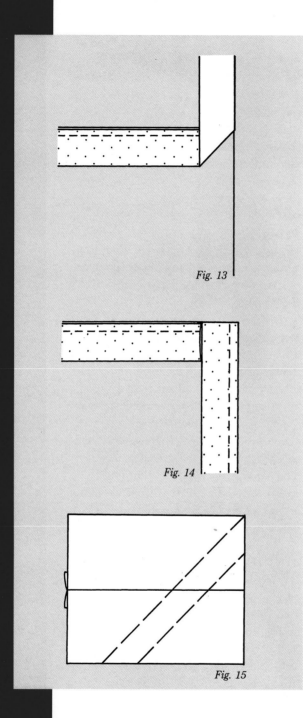

Fig. 13

Fig. 14

Fig. 15

Using the usual seam allowance, and starting 10 cm (4 in) from the beginning of the binding, sew the binding to the quilt through all three layers. Do not pull the binding or your quilt will have small gathers. Sew to within the seam allowance from the next corner. Back stitch and remove the quilt from the machine. Fold the binding up and away from the quilt as shown (Fig. 13), then fold it down over itself to form a pleat at the corner (Fig. 14). Recommence sewing at the edge where the pleat is formed and continue around the quilt. When you get back to the start, tuck the end of the binding into the fold of the start of the binding and finish sewing. Turn the binding over to the back of the quilt and slipstitch it down. Neatly fold the corners to match the front, as you sew down the binding.

Occasionally, you may have a long narrow strip left over from the border fabric for the binding. You can cut a straight binding from this, or you can cut the strip in half and rejoin the halves with a small stitch and matching thread. Press the seam open. The fabric will then be wide enough to cut bias binding strips (Fig. 15).

LABELLING

Your quilt is not finished unless you label it. Commercial labels are available, as are stamps, but I prefer a hand-sewn label that should include, at a minimum, your name, the date the quilt was finished, and the reason for it being made.

Make it easy for the curators of the future when they catalogue your classic quilt!

**From top:
Happy Birthday,
Scrap Sunburst and
Wild Goose Chase**

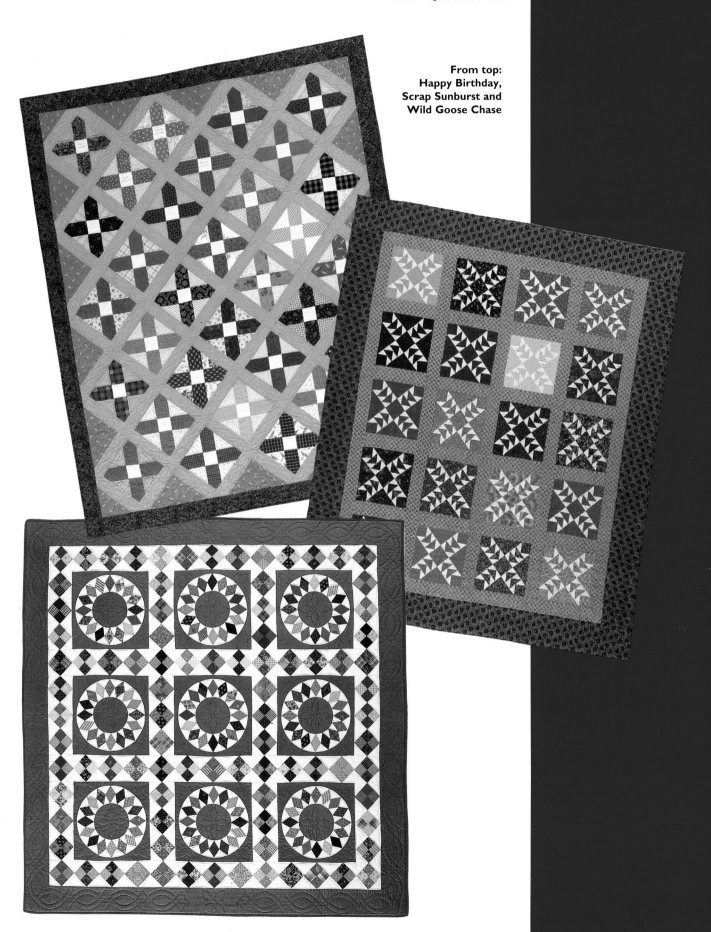

The Quilts

My inspiration for quilts to make comes from my many books on antique quilts – in particular, scrap quilts. I enjoy the challenge of studying the design and turning the patterns into template-free methods.

In selecting the quilts for this book, I have chosen fourteen of my favourites from literally thousands of designs and there are endless variations possible from the chosen designs. Having spent a year completing these quilts, I find that for every one completed, many others have become part of my thoughts, ready to be realised some time in the future.

Unlike the quiltmakers of the past, we have the pleasure of working with the colours, textures and designs without the necessity of producing a practical object. With the shortcuts and modern techniques described in this book, we can do it to satisfy our desire to create something of lasting beauty.

Often it is not the finished article that gives the greatest pleasure. The adaptation of an old block, the selection of the fabrics and the making of the quilt are all separate and distinctive pleasures. I hope you get as much satisfaction from making these quilts as I did.

Some of you will produce quilts similar to those in the book. Others will adapt the blocks, size, colours and fabrics to their own tastes. The thought that my book has inspired the making of these quilts would give me much satisfaction. I hope you will share your quilts with me.

Almost Amish

YOU WILL NEED

- ■ 1.2 m (1 1/3 yd) of beige fabric
- ■ 1 m (1 1/8 yd) of blue fabric
- ■ 75 cm (30 in) of red fabric
- ■ 1.75 m (2 yd) of fabric for the backing
- ■ 30 cm (12 in) of fabric for the binding
- ■ 130 cm (50 in) square of wadding
- ■ sewing machine
- ■ rotary cutter and mat
- ■ large and small quilter's rulers
- ■ 100% cotton thread
- ■ quilting thread
- ■ quilting needles
- ■ quilting hoop
- ■ water-soluble marker pen
- ■ usual sewing supplies

Right: Detail of 'Almost Amish'

Although the Amish women were not quiltmakers when they migrated to America, it was not long before they were following in their English neighbours' footsteps. By simplifying commonly used blocks, using only plain fabrics, and adding large borders, the distinctive Amish quilt evolved. Many 'Double Irish Chain' quilts were made and heavily quilted by the Amish.

This wallhanging will not take long to piece, and will give you plenty of room to practise your hand-quilting.

Machine-pieced, hand-quilted
Finished size: 125 cm (48 in) square
Block size: 31.5 cm (12 1/4 in)

CUTTING
From the red fabric
Cut eleven 6 cm (2 1/4 in) wide strips; cut one of these strips into three 35 cm (14 in) long pieces and another strip into two 54 cm (21 in) long pieces.

From the blue fabric
1. Cut fourteen 6 cm (2 1/4 in) wide strips; cut one of these strips into three 35 cm (14 in) long pieces.
2. Cut four 14 cm (5 in) squares.

From the beige fabric
1. Cut two 6 cm (2 1/4 in) wide strips; cut one of these strips into three 35 cm (14 in) long pieces.
2. Cut one 15 cm (5 3/4 in) wide strip.
3. Cut four 24 cm (9 1/4 in) squares.
4. Cut four 14 cm (5 in) wide strips for the borders.

CONSTRUCTION
1. Sew seven long strips together in the order shown to make section A (Fig. 1). Make one.
2. Sew seven long strips together in the order shown to make section B (Fig. 2). Make one.
3. Sew seven long strips together in the order shown to make section C (Fig. 3). Make one.
4. Sew the 35 cm (14 in) long strips together in the order shown to make section D (Fig. 4). Make one.
5. From sections A, B, and C, cut ten 6 cm (2 1/4 in) wide strips (Fig. 5). From section D, cut five 6 cm (2 1/4 in) wide strips in the same way.
6. Join these crosscut sections into blocks as shown (Fig. 6). Make five blocks.
7. For the alternate blocks, sew one blue strip to both sides of a 15 cm (5 3/4 in) beige strip to make section E (Fig. 7). Make one.
8. From section E, cut eight 6 cm (2 1/4 in) strips.
9. To the remainder of section E, sew one 54 cm (21 in) long strip of red, to both sides, as shown, to make section F (Fig. 8). Make one section F.

ALMOST AMISH

QUICK TIP

For this wallhanging, use Pellon or another low-loft wadding. This will help you to make smaller quilting stitches, if you are hand-quilting.

10 From section F, cut off eight 6 cm (2¼ in) wide strips.

11 Sew one section E to opposite sides of a 24 cm (9¼ in) square (Fig. 9). Sew one strip cut from section F to the two remaining sides of the square (Fig. 10).

12 Join the blocks together in three rows of three (Fig. 11).

For the borders

1 Cut four border pieces the same length as the pieced centre. Attach two borders to opposite sides of the quilt.

2 Sew a blue square to both ends of the remaining border pieces, then attach them to the quilt.

TO FINISH

1 From the backing fabric, cut two 20 cm (8 in) wide strips across the width of the fabric. Join them at one short end. From this long strip, cut a 135 cm (53 in) long strip. Sew this to one side of the remaining backing fabric.

2 Spread the backing fabric on a large work surface with the wrong side up. Centre the wadding on the backing and trim off the excess backing. Smooth out any wrinkles. Place the quilt top on the wadding, face upwards, and smooth again. Pin, then baste the layers together.

3 Mark the quilting pattern. Secure the quilt in the hoop and hand-quilt it in designs of your choice. (I quilted diagonally through the small squares, then quilted a feathered circle in the plain blocks and a cable pattern in the borders.)

4 From the binding fabric, cut four 5 cm (2 in) wide strips across the width of the fabric. Bind the quilt, following the general instructions on pages 13–14.

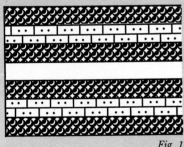

Fig. 1

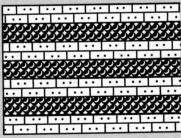

Fig. 2

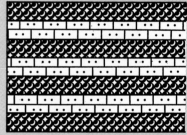

Fig. 3

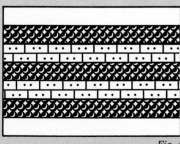

Fig. 4

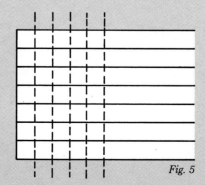

Fig. 5

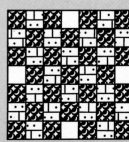

Fig. 6

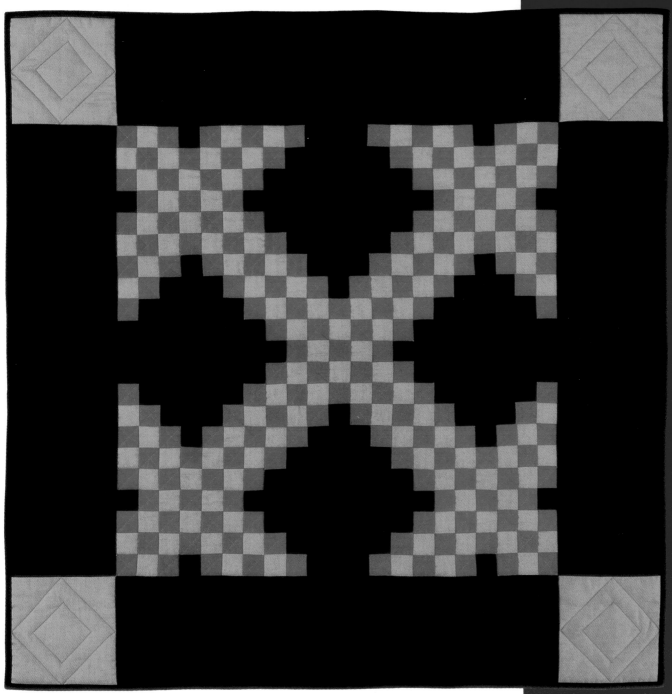

'Almost Amish' variation

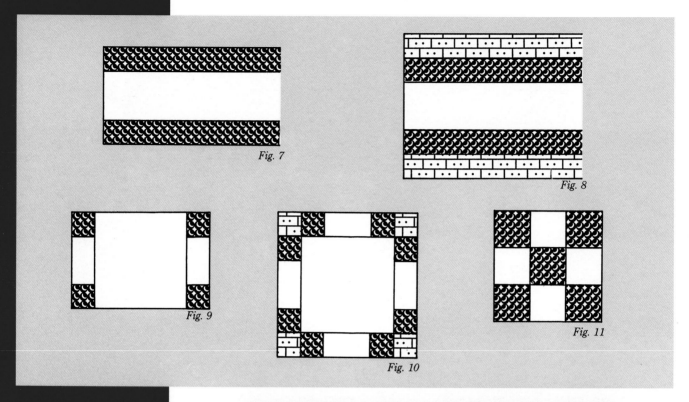

Fig. 7

Fig. 8

Fig. 9

Fig. 10

Fig. 11

Above: Detail of the quilting on 'Almost Amish'

Wild Goose Chase

In most of my books on old quilts, this pattern usually occurs using only two colours. For this quilt, I have chosen strong colours with an old-fashioned look. The contrast with the brown lattice strips and borders gives a unique look to this once commonly made quilt.

Machine-pieced,
professionally machine-quilted
Finished size: 165 cm × 198 cm
(65 in × 78 in)
Block size: 25 cm (10 in)

CUTTING
From the print fabrics
1 Cut one 18.5 cm (7^{1}/4 in) square, then cut each square twice, diagonally, to yield four triangles.
2 Cut one 8.5 cm (3^{1}/4 in) square.
3 Cut four 6.5 cm (2^{1}/2 in) squares.
4 Cut two 10.5 cm (4 in) squares, then cut each square twice, diagonally, to yield eight triangles.

From the light-coloured fabric
Cut fourteen 6 cm (2^{1}/4 in) wide strips. Cut them into 240 squares, then cut them once, diagonally, to yield 480 triangles.

From the lattice fabric
Cutting along the length of the fabric, cut eleven 7.5 cm (3 in) wide strips. Cut four of these strips into sixteen 7.5 cm × 26.5 cm (3 in × 10^{1}/2 in) rectangles.

From the border fabric
Cutting along the length of the fabric, cut four 16.5 cm (6^{1}/2 in) wide strips.

CONSTRUCTION
For each block
1 Sew two light-coloured fabric triangles to the short sides of a print fabric small triangle to make an A unit (Fig. 1). Make eight.
2 Sew the A units into pairs to make a B unit (Fig. 2). Make four.
3 Sew two light-coloured fabric triangles to the sides of a print fabric small square to make a C unit (Fig. 3). Make four.

YOU WILL NEED
- **1.75 m (2 yd) of brown fabric for the lattice strips**
- **1.75 m (2 yd) of fabric for the outer borders and binding**
- **1 m (1^{1}/2 yd) of light-coloured fabric**
- **20 cm (8 in) of twenty different print fabrics**
- **3.5 m (4 yd) of fabric for the backing**
- **double-bed size wadding (medium or low-loft)**
- **rotary cutter and mat**
- **large and small quilter's rulers**
- **sewing machine**
- **100% cotton thread**
- **usual sewing supplies**

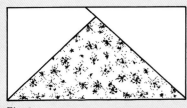

Fig. 1
A unit

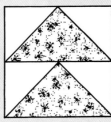

Fig. 2
B unit

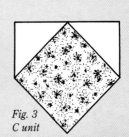

Fig. 3
C unit

QUICK TIP
By making more blocks and omitting the lattice strips, you can give another new look to an old pattern.

4   Sew one C unit to one B unit to make a D unit (Fig. 4). Make four.

5   Sew print fabric large triangles to the opposite sides of a D unit to make an E unit (Fig. 5). Make two.

6   Sew the remaining D units to the opposite sides of the 8.5 cm (3¼ in) print fabric squares to make an F unit (Fig. 6). Make one.

7   Sew one E unit to the opposite sides of an F unit to complete the block (Fig. 7).

8   Make twenty blocks in the same way, using a different print fabric for making each one.

ASSEMBLING

1   Arrange the blocks together in four vertical rows of five blocks each. Join the blocks with a length of sashing in between each one.

2   Measure the length of the rows and cut five lattice strips to this length. Pin the centre of the lattice strip to the centre of a row, then pin the ends together. Pin the whole length, then sew. Join all the rows and lattice strips in this way. Attach lattice strips to both sides of the joined blocks in the same way.

3   Measure the width of the quilt top and cut two lattice strips to this length. Pin and sew them to the top and bottom of the quilt top.

4   Measure, cut and join the outer borders in the same way as the long lattice strips. Attach the borders, following the general directions for borders on page 11.

TO FINISH

1   Cut the backing fabric in half across the width and remove the selvages. Join the two pieces along one long side. This seam will go across the quilt.

2   Spread the backing, wrong side up, on a large work surface. Centre the wadding on the backing and smooth out any wrinkles. Place the quilt top on the wadding, face upwards, and smooth again. Pin the three layers together ready for quilting.

3   This quilt was professionally machine-quilted in an all-over design. If you prefer, you could outline-quilt by hand, 7.5 mm (¼ in) from the seams on the light-coloured fabric, and quilt a cable-style design in the borders.

4   Cut four straight 5.5 cm (2¼ in) binding strips down the length of the remaining border fabric or cut and join eight bias strips, as instructed in the general instructions for binding on pages 13–14. Bind the edges of the quilt.

Above: Detail of a block

WILD GOOSE CHASE

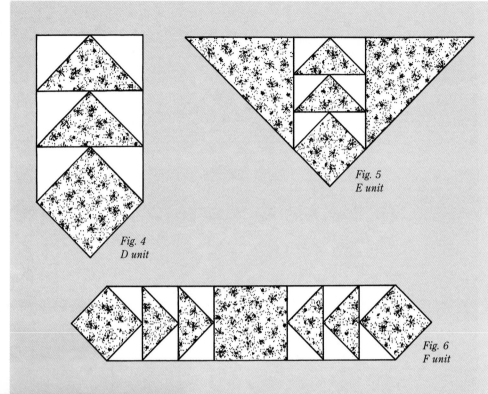

Fig. 4
D unit

Fig. 5
E unit

Fig. 6
F unit

Fig. 7

Above: Detail of 'Wild Goose Chase'

Little Red

Baskets have always been among my favourite quilt designs. Feeling rather guilty about the amount of red fabric I had stored, I decided to make a quick-and-easy basket quilt. (Although I am very pleased with the result, I did not make much of a dent in the red fabrics!) I have placed the blocks in a manner very common to traditional basket and other one-way block quilts. This layout was used in earlier times when many beds were placed up against a wall and the quilt could be admired from the side.

Machine-pieced, hand-quilted
Finished size: 160 cm (63 in) square
Block size: 16 cm (6 in)

CUTTING
From the background fabric
1 Cut seven 5.5 cm (2 in) wide strips. Cut them into seventy-two 5.5 cm × 9.5 cm (2 in × 3 1/2 in) rectangles.
2 Cut two 10.5 cm (3 7/8 in) wide strips. Cut them into eighteen 10.5 cm (3 7/8 in) squares, then cut the squares once, diagonally, to yield thirty-six triangles.
3 Cut seven 6.5 cm (2 3/8 in) wide strips. Cut them into 108 squares, 6.5 cm (2 3/8 in), then cut the squares once, diagonally, to yield 216 triangles.

From each of the red scraps
1 Cut one 14.5 cm (5 3/8 in) square. Cut the square once, diagonally, to yield two triangles.
2 Cut five 6.5 cm (2 3/8 in) squares. Cut them once, diagonally, to yield ten triangles.

From the border and plain block fabric
1 Cut four strips, 11.5 cm × 170 cm (4 1/2 in × 65 in) down the length of fabric. Set them aside for the borders.

2 Cut twenty-five 17.5 cm (6 1/2 in) squares.
3 Cut two 14 cm (5 1/4 in) squares. Cut them once, diagonally, to yield four corner triangles.
4 Cut five 26.5 cm (9 3/4 in) squares. Cut them twice diagonally to yield twenty side triangles.

CONSTRUCTION
For each block
1 Sew three small triangles to three background triangles to make three squares (Fig. 1).
2 Join the squares together with background triangles as shown in figure 2. Join these sections to form the top of the basket as shown in figure 3.
3 Sew the top of the basket to the red basket triangle (Fig. 4).
4 Sew a small basket triangle to two background rectangles (Fig. 5). Place the triangles facing in opposite directions.

YOU WILL NEED
- 25 cm (10 in) squares of eighteen different red fabrics
- 1.2 m (1 1/3 yd) of light-coloured fabric for the background
- 2.5 m (2 3/4 yd) of red fabric for the plain blocks and borders
- 3.5 m (4 yd) of fabric for the backing
- 165 cm (65 in) square of wadding
- sewing machine
- 100% cotton thread
- rotary cutter and mat
- large and small quilter's rulers
- quilting hoop
- quilting needles
- quilting thread
- water-soluble marker pen

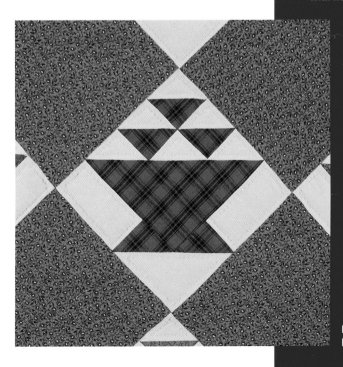

Left: Detail of a Basket block

QUICK TIP
If you do not have enough fabrics of the same colour, the quilt looks very attractive if each basket is a different colour. This variation is called 'Scrap Baskets' and would make an ideal friendship quilt.

5 Sew the pieces made in step 4 to the sides of the basket, then sew a 10.5 cm ($3^{7}/8$ in) triangle to the bottom of the block (Fig. 6). Make thirty-six blocks.

ASSEMBLING

1 Sew the side triangles, plain blocks and Basket blocks together into rows as shown in the construction diagram.
2 Join the rows together, then add the corner triangles to complete the centre.

For the borders

1 Measure the width of the quilt top and cut two of the reserved border strips to this length. Matching the centre of the border to the centre of the quilt top, and matching the ends, pin and sew the borders to the top and bottom of the quilt top.
2 Measure the length of the quilt top, including the attached borders. Cut and sew the side borders in the same way as for the top and bottom borders.

TO FINISH

1 Cut the backing fabric in half across the width and remove the selvages. Join the two pieces along one long side. Lay the backing, face down, on a large work surface. Centre the wadding on the backing and smooth out any wrinkles. Place the quilt top on the wadding, face upwards, and smooth again. Pin and baste the layers together.
2 This quilt is hand-quilted 7.5 mm ($^{1}/4$ in) from the seams in all the light areas and diagonal lines in the borders. In the plain blocks, this quilt was quilted in a traditional design, using a commercial stencil. Mark the quilting pattern as you go and remove all the pen lines when you have finished quilting for the day.
3 From the remaining border fabric, cut four straight 5.5 cm ($2^{1}/4$ in) wide strips for the binding, or cut and join bias strips, if you prefer. Attach the binding, following the general instructions for binding on pages 13–14.

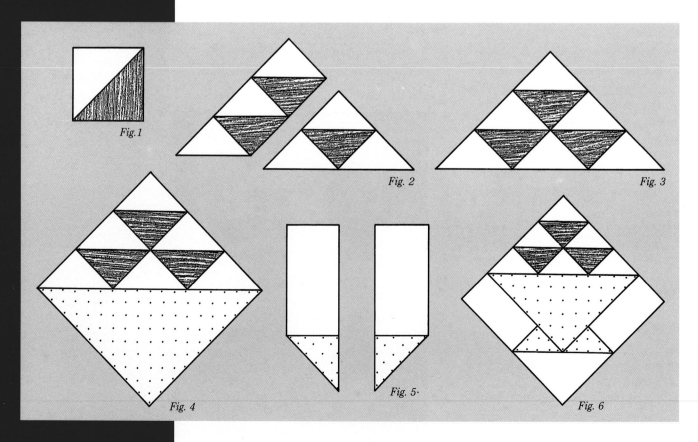

Fig.1

Fig. 2

Fig. 3

Fig. 4

Fig. 5

Fig. 6

LITTLE RED

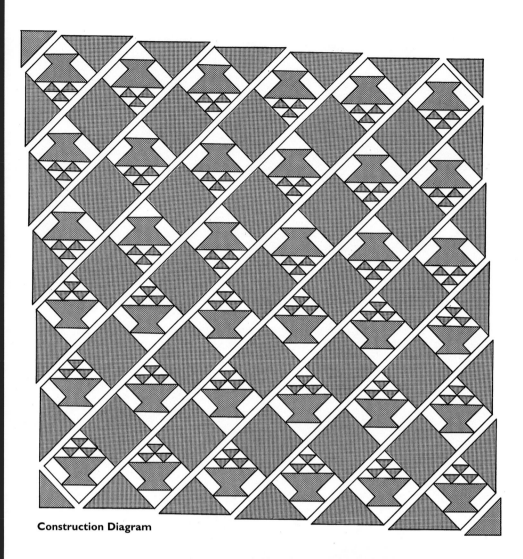

Construction Diagram

Left: Detail of 'Little Red'

'Little Red' variation

Not So Crazy

YOU WILL NEED

- a good supply of fabric scraps – including checks, geometrics, spots and stripes – approximately 2.5 m (2³/4 yd) in total

Note: Packs of squares from quilt shops are ideal for this quilt. Most quilt shops also sell fat eighths of suitable materials.

- 1.6 m (1³/4 yd) of fabric for the borders (this includes fabric for the binding)
- 3.25 m (3¹/2 yd) of fabric for the backing
- 160 cm (64 in) square of low-loft wadding or a piece of flannel
- rotary cutter and mat
- large and small quilter's rulers
- quilting hoop
- sewing machine
- 100% cotton thread
- crochet cotton, stranded cotton, or similar, for tying
- large darning needle
- usual sewing supplies

In the early pioneer days of North America, many quilts were needed for warmth in the harsh climate experienced by the intrepid settlers. A number of these quilts were randomly pieced and usually tied. The fabrics used did not always lend themselves to fine quilting, and the women did not have the time to devote to needlework. Utility was a greater consideration than decoration. These utility quilts were covered by the best quilt that the family possessed. Once necessity was satisfied, the quilter could devote more time to the art of quilting. My 'Not So Crazy' quilt is a tribute to these women who worked so hard to keep their families warm.

Machine-pieced, tied
Finished size: 150 cm (60 in) square
Block size: 25 cm (10 in)

CUTTING

From the scrap fabrics

1 Cut fifty 7.5 cm x 14 cm (3 in x 5¹/2 in) rectangles.
2 Cut fifty 10.5 cm (4 in) squares.
3 Cut fifty 6.5 cm (2¹/2 in) squares.
4 Cut twenty-five 8.5 cm x 10.5 cm (4 in x 3¹/2 in) rectangles.
5 Cut twenty-five 11.5 cm (4¹/2 in) squares.
6 Cut twenty-five 12.5 cm (4⁷/8 in) squares. Cut these squares once, diagonally, to yield fifty triangles.

From the border fabric

Cut four 18 cm (6¹/2 in) wide strips down the length of the fabric.

CONSTRUCTION

1 Sew all the 7.5 cm x 14 cm (3 in x 5¹/2 in) rectangles into pairs to make A units (Fig. 1). Make sure you do not sew two of the same fabric together.

2 Sew all the triangles into pairs to make twenty-five 11.5 cm (4¹/2 in) squares. Sew one of these squares to one of the 11.5 cm (4¹/2 in) squares (Fig. 2).
3 Sew all the 6.5 cm (2¹/2 in) squares to the top of the rectangles made in step 2 to form B units (Fig. 3).
4 Sew all the 10.5 cm (4 in) squares together into pairs. Sew one 8.5 cm x 10.5 cm (3¹/2 in x 4 in) rectangle to the top of the pair of squares to form C units (Fig. 4).
5 Sew the A, B and C units together to form the block (Fig. 5). Make twenty-five blocks.

ASSEMBLING

1 Lay the blocks out in five rows of five blocks. Do not place them all the same way, but move the blocks around until the fabric colours are evenly distributed and you are satisfied with the arrangement.
2 Sew the blocks together into rows. Sew the rows together to form the quilt top.

For the borders

1 Measure the width of the quilt top and cut two of the 18 cm (6¹/2 in) wide reserved strips to this length. Pin, matching the centres and ends. Attach the borders to the top and bottom of the quilt top, following the general instructions for borders on page 11.
2 Measure the length of the quilt top, including the attached borders, then cut and attach the side borders in the same way as the top and bottom borders.

TO FINISH

1 Cut the backing fabric in half and remove the selvages. Join the two pieces along the long side. Lay the backing, face

NOT SO CRAZY

QUICK TIP

'Do-it-yourself Crazy': To make your own original block, start by drawing on graph paper a square of the required size. Break this square down into some simple shapes (about six different shapes that can be repeated is ideal). Measure these shapes and add seam allowances. Some other shapes I have used are shown in figures 6 and 7.

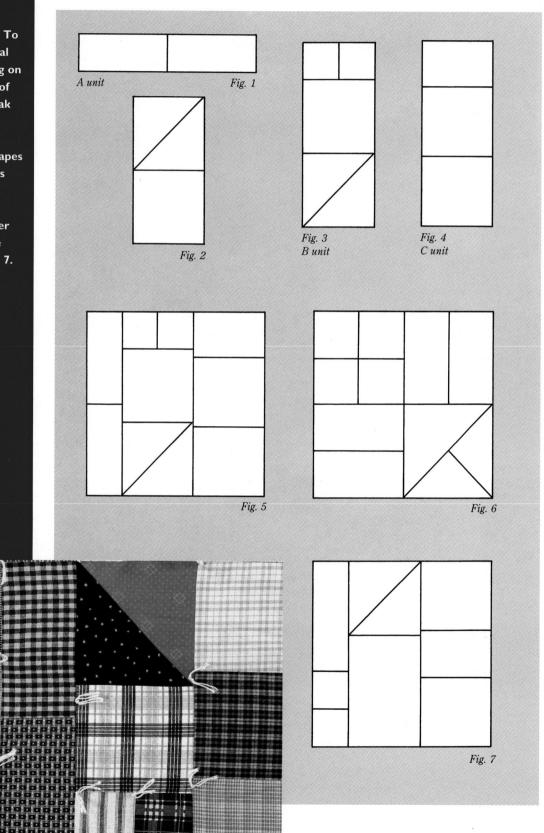

A unit   Fig. 1

Fig. 2

Fig. 3
B unit

Fig. 4
C unit

Fig. 5

Fig. 6

Fig. 7

Right: Detail of one 'Not So Crazy' block

down, on a large work surface. Centre the wadding or flannel on top, approximately 8 cm (3 in) in from the edges. Trim off the excess backing and smooth out any wrinkles. Place the quilt top on the wadding, face upwards, and smooth again. Pin and baste the three layers together ready for tying.

2 I tied this quilt using crochet cotton. If you prefer to quilt, a big quilting stitch would work very well on this quilt.

3 From the remaining border fabric, cut four 7.5 cm (3 in) strips down the length of the fabric for the binding. Bind the quilt, following the general instructions on pages 13–14.

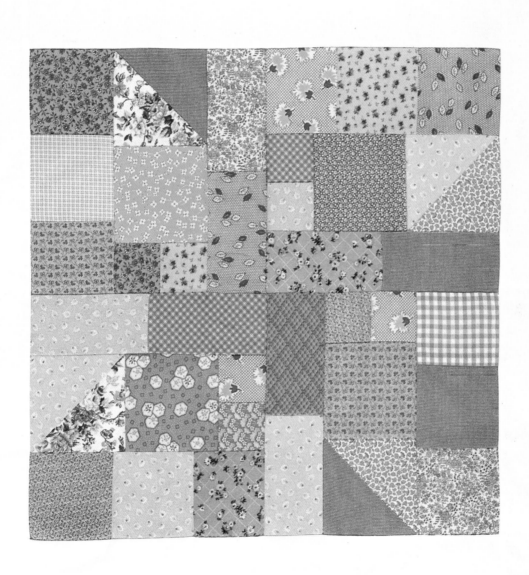

'Not So Crazy' variation

Turkey Tracks

YOU WILL NEED

- 1 m (1¹/8 yd) of white print fabric for the background
- 60 cm (24 in) of red print fabric
- 60 cm (24 in) of yellow print fabric
- 2.25 m (2¹/2 yd) of blue print fabric (includes fabric for the binding)
- 3.25 m (3¹/2 yd) of fabric for the backing
- 1.5 m (1²/3 yd) square of medium- or low-loft wadding
- sewing machine
- 100% cotton sewing thread
- rotary cutter and mat
- large and small quilter's rulers
- quilting hoop
- quilting needle
- quilting thread, Navy
- usual sewing supplies
- water-soluble marker pen

This quilt pattern, known by many other names including Goose Tracks, Fanny's Fan, Sage Bud and Fancy Flowers, is one that I love. This quilt was inspired by a photograph I saw, with this particular pattern only partly shown. It caught my imagination, and I knew I had to make it.

Machine-pieced, hand-quilted
Finished size: 148 cm (58 in) square
Block size: 25 cm (10 in)

CUTTING

From the white print fabric

1 Cut two 8.5 cm (3¹/4 in) wide strips. Cut them into twenty-six squares, then cut each square twice, diagonally, to yield 104 triangles.
2 Cut ten 6.5 cm (2¹/2 in) wide strips. Cut six of these strips into fifty-two 6.5 cm x 11.5 cm (2¹/2 in x 4¹/2 in) rectangles. Cut the remaining strips into fifty-two 6.5 cm (2¹/2 in) squares.

From the red print fabric

1 Cut six 4 cm (1¹/2 in) wide strips. Cut two of these strips into fifty-two 4 cm (1¹/2 in) squares.
2 Cut one 6.5 cm (2¹/2 in) wide strip. Cut the strip into thirteen 6.5 cm (2¹/2 in) squares.
3 Cut three 5 cm (1⁷/8 in) wide strips. Cut them into fifty-two 5 cm (1⁷/8 in) squares, then cut the squares once, diagonally, to yield 104 triangles.

From the yellow print fabric

1 Cut four 4 cm (1¹/2 in) wide strips.
2 Cut six 5 cm (1⁷/8 in) wide strips. Cut them into one hundred and four 5 cm (1⁷/8 in) squares. Cut the squares once, diagonally, to yield 208 triangles.

From the blue print fabric

1 Cut one 40 cm (17 in) wide strip. Set it aside for the binding.
2 Cut two 7.5 cm (2⁷/8 in) wide strips. Cut them into twenty-six 7.5 cm (2⁷/8 in) squares, then cut the squares once, diagonally, to yield fifty-two triangles.
3 From the length of the fabric, cut twelve 26.5 cm (10¹/2 in) squares.
4 Cut four 10.5 cm (4 in) wide strips. Set them aside for the borders.

CONSTRUCTION

1 Sew two white print rectangles to the opposite sides of the red 6.5 cm (2¹/2 in) squares to make A units (Fig. 1).
2 Sew a red print and yellow print triangle to both sides of a white print triangle. Make fifty-four with the red print on the left side and fifty-four with the yellow print on the left side to make B units (Fig. 2).
3 Sew a 4 cm (1¹/2 in) wide red print strip to a 4 cm (1¹/2 in) wide yellow print strip. Make four pairs (Fig. 3). Cut the joined strips into 104 Two-patch pieces.
4 Sew a yellow print triangle to two sides of a 4 cm (1¹/2 in) red print square to make a C unit (Fig. 4). Make fifty-four.
5 Sew a blue print triangle to the long side of the C unit to make a D unit (Fig. 5). Make fifty-two.

TURKEY TRACKS

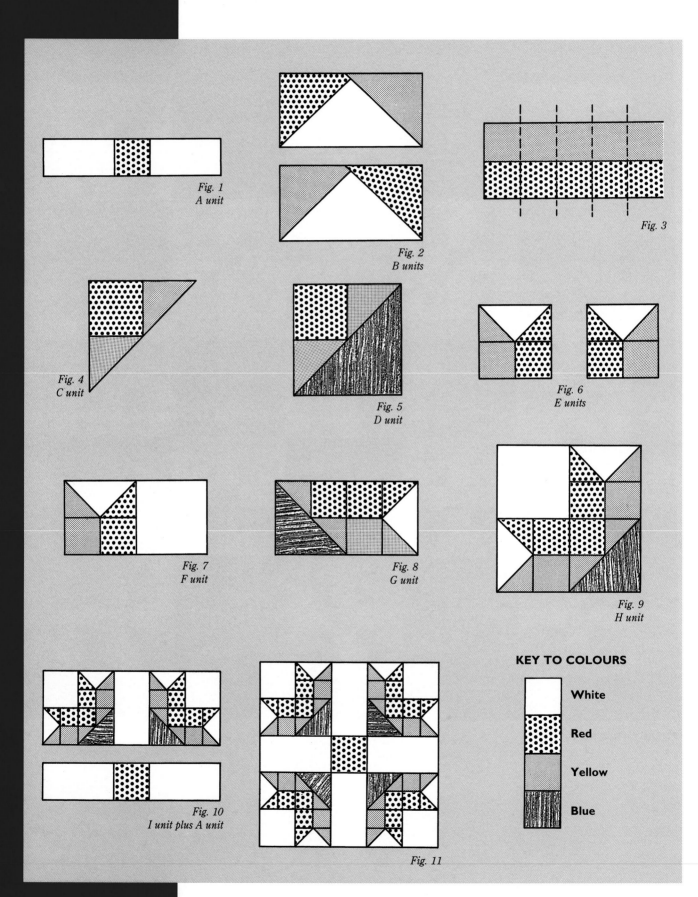

Fig. 1
A unit

Fig. 2
B units

Fig. 3

Fig. 4
C unit

Fig. 5
D unit

Fig. 6
E units

Fig. 7
F unit

Fig. 8
G unit

Fig. 9
H unit

Fig. 10
I unit plus A unit

Fig. 11

KEY TO COLOURS

White

Red

Yellow

Blue

6 Sew the Two-patch pieces to the B units to make E units, matching colours as shown (Fig. 6). Make fifty-two of each colour way.

7 Sew a white print square to each of the fifty-two E units, with the red print on the right-hand side to make F units (Fig. 7).

8 Sew a D unit to the remaining E Unit to make a G unit (Fig. 8).

9 Sew a G unit and an F unit together to make an H unit (Fig. 9). Make fifty-two.

10 Join two H units with a white print rectangle between them to make an I unit (Fig. 10). Make twenty-six. Join two I units with an A unit to complete the block (Fig. 11). Make thirteen blocks.

ASSEMBLING

Lay out the pieced blocks and the blue print squares. Sew them together into rows. Sew the rows together.

For the borders

1 Measure the width of the quilt top and cut two of the reserved border strips to this length. Pin the borders to the top and bottom of the quilt top, matching the centres and ends. Stitch.

2 Measure the length of the quilt top, including the attached borders. Cut, pin and sew the two side borders in the same way as the top and bottom borders.

TO FINISH

1 Cut the backing fabric in half across the width and remove the selvages. Join the pieces together along the long side. This seam will go across the quilt.

2 Lay the backing face down on a large work surface. Centre the wadding on top, approximately 8 cm (3 in) from the edges. Trim any excess backing and smooth out any wrinkles. Place the quilt top on top of the wadding, face upwards, and smooth again. Pin and baste the layers together.

3 I quilted 7.5 mm ($^1/_4$ in) from the seams in all the white areas and used a commercial stencil for the blue blocks and the borders. Mark the quilting pattern as you go and remove all the pen lines when you have finished quilting for the day.

4 From the fabric set aside for the binding, cut seven 5.5 cm ($2^1/_2$ in) wide straight strips across the width. Join the strips with diagonal seams. Bind the quilt, following the general instructions for binding on pages 13–14.

QUICK TIP
By placing the blocks on point, you will have an interesting variation. This pattern also lends itself to a single-block wallhanging.

Above: Detail of a 'Turkey Tracks' block

Milky Way

YOU WILL NEED

- 3.5 m (4 yd) of blue fabric (this includes fabric for the binding)
- 3 m (3¼ yd) of white fabric
- 4 m (4½ yd) of fabric for the backing
- 190 cm (75 in) square of medium- or low-loft wadding
- rotary cutter and mat
- large and small quilter's rulers
- 100% cotton thread
- sewing machine
- usual sewing supplies

Blue and white quilts are always popular. Here is a simple design, using just squares and triangles, to make a traditional blue and white quilt to add to your own collection.

Machine-pieced,
professionally machine-quilted
Finished size: 187 cm (73½ in) square

CUTTING

From the blue fabric

1 Cut nine strips 6 cm (2¼ in) wide.
2 Cut eleven strips 10.5 cm (4 in) wide. Cut three of these strips into thirty squares and cut two more squares from another strip for a total of thirty-two squares. The remaining strips will be used for borders.
3 Cut eight strips 11.5 cm (4³/8 in) wide. Cut them into seventy-two squares, then cut the squares once, diagonally, to yield 144 triangles.

From the white fabric

1 Cut nine strips 6 cm (2¼ in) wide.
2 Cut eleven strips 10.5 cm (4 in) wide. Cut three of these strips into thirty squares and cut two more squares from another strip for a total of thirty-two squares. The remaining strips will be used for borders.
3 Cut eight strips 11.5 cm (4³/8 in) wide. Cut them into seventy-two squares, then cut the squares once, diagonally, to yield 144 triangles.

CONSTRUCTION

1 Sew all the 6 cm (2¼ in) wide blue and white strips into pairs (Fig. 1).
2 Cut the pairs of strips into 162 sections 6 cm (2¼ in) long. Rejoin these sections to make Four-patch blocks (Fig. 2).
3 Sew all the blue triangles to all the white triangles, as shown in figure 3, to make seventy-two squares.

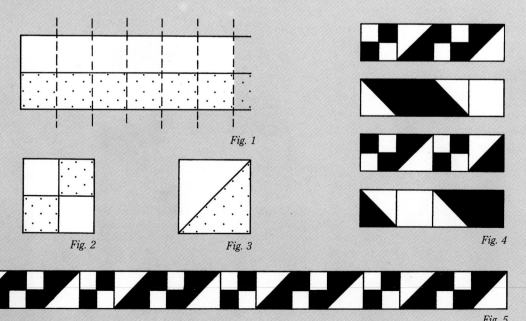

Fig. 1

Fig. 2

Fig. 3

Fig. 4

Fig. 5

MILKY WAY

Above: Detail of 'Milky Way'

Above: The same pattern, pieced in a variety of print fabrics, creates a whole new look.

4 Using the Four-patch blocks, plain squares and half-square triangles, assemble sixteen blocks as shown (Fig. 4).

ASSEMBLING

1 Following the construction diagram, join the blocks together in four rows of four blocks.

2 Make one row as shown in figure 5. Attach it to the bottom of the quilt.

3 Make the right-hand side border as shown in the construction diagram. Attach it to the right-hand side of the quilt.

For the borders

1 Join the remaining blue strips together into one long strip. Measure across the width of the quilt and cut two strips this length. Pin, then sew them to the top and bottom of the quilt, matching centres and the ends. Measure the length of the quilt and cut two strips this length. Pin and sew them to the sides of the quilt in the same way as for the top and bottom borders.

2 Join the remaining white strips into a long strip. Measure, cut and sew the white border as for the blue border.

Construction Diagram

QUICK TIP
When using your rulers for cutting out, make sure the printed side of the ruler is in contact with the fabric. This prevents errors in size caused by parallax error (or sighting at an angle through the ruler).

TO FINISH

1 Cut the backing fabric in half across the width and remove the selvages. Join the pieces along one long side. Lay the backing fabric face down on a large work surface. Centre the wadding on top and smooth out any wrinkles. Lay the quilt top on the wadding, face upwards, and smooth again. Pin the three layers together securely.

2 This quilt was professionally machine-quilted in an all-over pattern. Should you decide to hand-quilt, a pattern such as Baptist's Fan would suit this quilt.

3 From the remainder of the blue fabric, cut seven 5.5 cm (2¹/4 in) wide bias strips. Join the strips with diagonal seams. Bind the quilt, following the general instructions on pages 13–14.

Old Bailey

YOU WILL NEED

- **50 cm (20 in) of fabric for the centre squares and first border**
- **total of 2 m (2¼ yd) of different light-coloured fabrics**
- **total of 3.5 m (4 yd) of different dark fabrics**
- **50 cm (20 in) of fabric for the binding**
- **3.5 m (4 yd) of fabric for the backing**
- **190 cm (75 in) of medium-loft wadding**
- **sewing machine**
- **100% cotton thread**
- **rotary cutter and mat**
- **large and small quilter's rulers**
- **large supply of safety pins**

By the mid-nineteenth century Log Cabin quilts were being made in their thousands. This popular design could use up tiny strips of fabrics, including cottons, wools, silks and even ribbons from cigar boxes.

Starting with a centre square (chimney) the light and dark strips are sewn around in as many rows as the maker desires. Overall designs are made by placing the blocks in light and dark combinations. In this quilt, the light and dark strips are sewn on opposite sides of the centre square in a variation known as 'Court House Steps'.

Machine-pieced,
professionally machine-quilted
Finished size: 160 cm × 182 cm (62 in × 72 in)
Block size: 24 cm (9½ in)

CUTTING
From the centre square fabric
Cut nine 5.5 cm (2 in) wide strips. Cut two of these strips into thirty squares. Separate these squares into two lots of fifteen.

From the light and dark fabrics
Cut the fabrics into 4 cm (1½ in) wide strips.

CONSTRUCTION
Note: Make fifteen blocks commencing with light strips and fifteen blocks commencing with dark strips.

1. Working on five blocks at a time and starting with light strips, sew five centre squares to a light strip (Fig. 1). Press the seams open and cut them apart as shown (Fig. 2).
2. Repeat on the opposite side of the square with a different light strip (Fig. 3). Press the seams outwards and cut them apart (Fig. 4).

3. Sew dark strips to the remaining sides of the square. Always make sure that different fabric strips are used. Press the seams outwards and cut the pieces apart. Continue in this manner until four light and four dark strips have been attached around the centre square to make block A (Fig. 5). Make fifteen A blocks.
4. Make fifteen B blocks, commencing with a dark fabric centre in the same way.

ASSEMBLING
Alternating A and B blocks, sew the blocks together in six rows of five blocks.

For the first border
1. Join the remaining 5.5 cm (2 in) strips of the centre square fabric into a long strip. Measure across the width of the quilt top and cut two strips this length. Pin and sew them to the top and bottom of the quilt top, matching centres and ends.
2. Measure the length of the quilt top, including the attached borders. Cut, pin and sew the side borders in the same way as the top and bottom borders.

For the pieced outer border
Cut a good mixture of dark strips and a few light strips into two hundred and forty-four 16.5 cm (6½ in) lengths. Make two borders of sixty strips each, and attach them to the sides of the quilt. Make two borders with sixty-two strips each, and attach them to the top and bottom of the quilt.

TO FINISH
1. Cut the backing fabric in half across the width and remove the selvages. Join the pieces together along the long side. This seam will go across the quilt.
2. Lay the backing face down on a large work surface. Centre the wadding on

OLD BAILEY

QUICK TIP

In this quilt, use up your smaller scraps first. For different effects, vary the colour combinations, and try using fabrics other than cotton. Every time you purchase fabric, buy a little more than you need, cut one strip off the end, and save it until you have sufficient strips for a Log Cabin quilt.

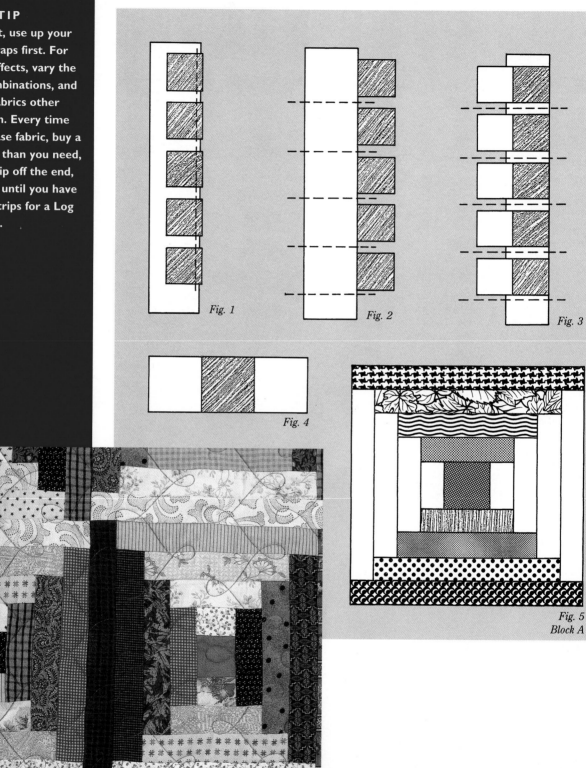

Fig. 1

Fig. 2

Fig. 3

Fig. 4

Fig. 5
Block A

Above: Detail of 'Old Bailey'

top, approximately 8 cm (3 in) from the edges. Trim any excess backing and smooth out any wrinkles. Place the quilt top on top of the wadding, face upwards, and smooth again. Pin and baste the layers together.

3 This quilt was professionally quilted by machine in an all-over continuous design.

4 From the fabric set aside for the binding, cut eight 5.5 cm (2¹/4 in) wide straight strips across the width of the fabric. Join the strips together with diagonal seams as these are less noticeable than straight seams. Bind the quilt, following the general instructions for binding on pages 13–14.

'Old Bailey' variation

Check Wedge

YOU WILL NEED

- **1.75 m (2 yd) of fabric for the background and borders**
- **good supply of checks and other fabric scraps (this is a great way to use up tiny odd-shaped pieces)**
- **1 m (1 1/8 yd) of soft fabric or a good quantity of junk mail for the foundation**
- **50 cm (20 in) of fabric for the binding**
- **2.75 m (3 yd) of fabric for the backing**
- **150 cm (60 in) square of medium-loft wadding**
- **sewing machine**
- **100% cotton thread**
- **rotary cutter and mat**
- **large and small quilter's rulers**
- **usual sewing supplies**

With the invention of the sewing machine, string-piecing or foundation-piecing became very popular. The tiniest of scraps could be sewn randomly onto paper and the shape required could then be cut out (the paper then being removed). Newspapers, old letters, and wrapping paper were commonly used for this purpose.

For this quilt I have used well-washed calico instead of paper. The instructions are the same for either method. However, if you choose paper, make your stitches smaller than usual. This will enable the paper to be easily removed later. The calico is NOT removed.

Machine-pieced, machine-quilted
Finished size: 150 cm (60 in) square

CUTTING
From the foundation (either fabric or paper)
Cut sixty-four 12 cm x 26 cm (4 1/2 in x 10 1/2 in) rectangles.

From the scraps
Cut the larger pieces of scraps into random-width strips. Smaller scraps need not be cut.

From the background fabric
1 From the length of the fabric, cut four 10 cm (4 in) wide strips, 160 cm (60 in) long and set them aside for the borders.
2 Cut four 11.5 cm (4 7/8 in) wide strips by the length of the fabric. Cut them into sixty 11.5 cm (4 7/8 in) squares.
3 Cut two more 11.5 cm (4 7/8 in) squares from the remainder of the fabric for a total of sixty-two squares. Cut the sixty-two squares once, diagonally, to yield 124 triangles.

CONSTRUCTION
For each block
1 Place one piece of scrap fabric on top of another with the raw edges matching down one side, and place them at an angle on the foundation (Fig. 1). Stitch.
2 Open out the top piece and continue stitching pieces over the previous piece, working towards each end of the foundation until it is completely covered (Fig. 2). Do not worry about trimming until all sixty-four foundations are covered. Press. With the wrong side facing, trim the foundation to 11.5 cm x 25 cm (4 in x 10 in).
3 From a plain piece of paper cut a 5.75 cm (2 in) square. Cut it once, diagonally, to make two triangles. Tape one of the triangles to your ruler, aligning the long side of the triangle to the ruler (Fig. 3).
4 Place the ruler over the pieced rectangle, matching the corner of the triangle to the corner of the rectangle (Fig. 4). Trim the corner of the rectangle. Repeat on all corners of the rectangle to form the wedge (Fig. 5).
5 Sew a background triangle to each side of the wedge to make sixty-four A units (Fig. 6).
6 If you are using a paper foundation, remove all the paper now. Sew four A units together to make one block (Fig. 7). Make sixteen blocks.

CHECK WEDGE

QUICK TIP

For an alternative binding, consider sewing strips of checked fabrics together, instead of using a single fabric. You will need a total length of 6 m (6¾ yd).

ASSEMBLING

Sew the blocks together in four rows of four blocks.

For the borders

1 Measure the width of the quilt top and cut two borders to this length. Pin the borders to the top and bottom of the quilt, matching the centres and the ends. Stitch.

2 Measure the length of the quilt top, including the attached borders. Pin and sew the side borders in the same way as for the top and bottom borders.

TO FINISH

1 Cut two 50 cm (20 in) pieces across the width of the backing fabric. Join them together along one short side and cut the length to match the length of the large backing piece. Join the two pieces.

2 Lay the backing face down on a large work surface. Centre the wadding on top, approximately 8 cm (3 in) from the edges. Trim any excess backing and smooth out any wrinkles. Place the quilt top on top of the wadding, face upwards, and smooth again. Pin and baste the layers together.

3 This quilt was commercially quilted in an all-over pattern. The design also lends itself well to tying or to hand-quilting.

4 From the fabric set aside for the binding, cut six 5 cm (2 in) wide straight strips across the width or ten bias strips the same width. Join the strips with diagonal seams as these are less noticeable than straight seams. Bind the quilt, following the general instructions for binding on pages 13–14.

Above: Detail of 'Check Wedge'

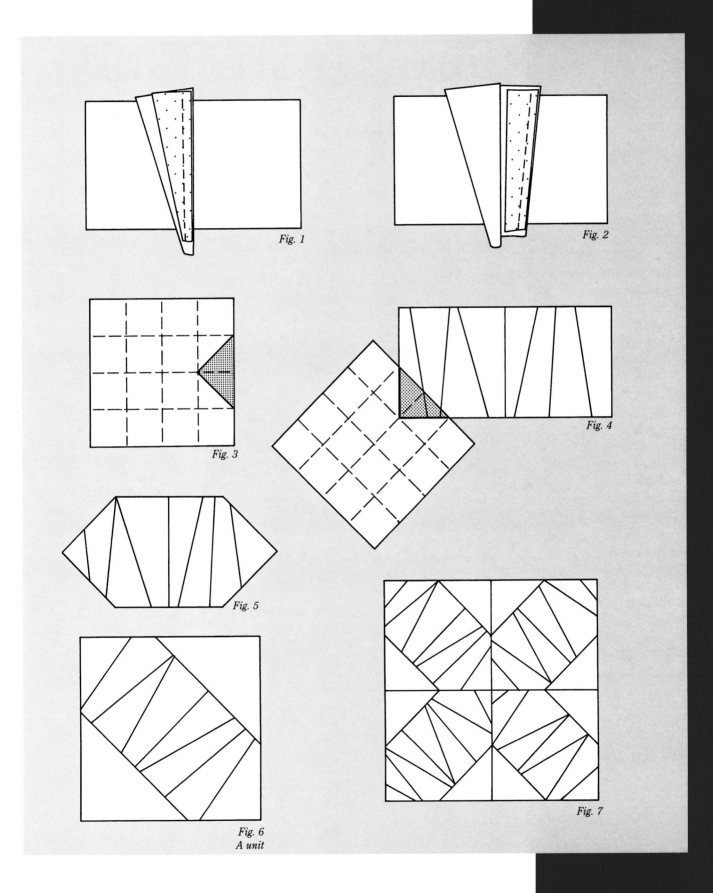

Fig. 1

Fig. 2

Fig. 3

Fig. 4

Fig. 5

Fig. 6
A unit

Fig. 7

The Quilt That Grew

YOU WILL NEED

- 2.25 m (2¹/₂ yd) of a large floral print for the main fabric
- 75 cm (30 in) each of two medium floral prints
- 30 cm (12 in) each of two small floral or other prints
- 70 cm (28 in) each of two small, light-coloured, open floral prints for the background
- 3.6 m (4 yd) of fabric for the backing
- 1.75 m (70 in) square of medium-loft wadding
- 40 cm (16 in) of fabric for the binding
- sewing machine
- walking foot (optional)
- 100% cotton thread
- rotary cutter and mat
- large and small quilter's rulers
- large supply of safety pins

The beautiful large floral prints available to quilters today lend themselves easily to the wonderful English-style medallion quilts, also known as border or frame quilts. I have made this quilt in memory of my English grandmother, Gran Low, who always sewed for other people. I am sure she would have loved this quilt.

Machine-pieced, machine-quilted
Finished size: 162 cm (66 in) square

CUTTING

1 From the background fabric, cut four 9 cm (3¹/₄ in) squares. Cut one 14 cm (5 in) square. Cut it twice, diagonally, to yield four triangles.
2 From the fabric used for the star, cut one 6.75 cm (2³/₈ in) wide strip. Fold the strip in half and make a cut at an angle of 45 degrees in one end. Make four cuts at the same angle, 6.75 cm (2³/₈ in) apart, to yield eight diamonds (Fig. 1).
3 From the large floral print, cut two 20.5 cm (7¹/₂ in) squares. Cut them once, diagonally, to yield four triangles.

CONSTRUCTION
For the centre star

1 Sew the diamonds together in pairs, leaving a 7.5 mm (¹/₄ in) seam allowance open at the top (Fig. 2).
2 Place a triangle on top of one diamond and begin sewing at the seam allowance line. Sew to the edge, then repeat on the other side to make an A unit (Fig. 3). Make four A units.
3 Sew two A units together, leaving the seam allowance open in the outer corner. Inset the corner squares making two B units (Fig. 4)
4 Join two B units, leaving the seam allowance open at both ends. Inset the last two squares (Fig. 5).
5 Sew a large floral triangle to each side of the star (Fig. 6).

For the first border

From the width of one of the small floral fabrics, cut two 3.5 cm (1¹/₂ in) wide strips. From one of these strips, cut two pieces 37.5 cm (13¹/₂ in) long. From the other strip, cut two pieces 41.5 cm (15¹/₂ in) long. Sew these strips to the star square.

For the second border (Hourglass)

1 From each of two different fabrics, cut twelve 11.5 cm (4¹/₄ in) squares. Cut them twice, diagonally, to yield forty-eight triangles. Place the triangles into light and dark pairs and chain-piece them together as shown (Fig. 7). Take care to keep the same piece (light or dark) on top for all the pairs.
2 Open out the triangles and fingerpress the seam to the dark side. Sew pairs of triangles together to make twenty-four Hourglass blocks (Fig. 8).
3 Join two rows of five blocks and two rows of seven blocks. Attach them to the star block. Measure all the sides to make sure they are equal.

For the third border

Cut three 3.5 cm (2 in) wide strips of your chosen fabric. Join them together at an angle of 45 degrees and press the seams open.

THE QUILT THAT GREW

QUICK TIP
If you wish, you can continue adding borders to make a much larger quilt than this one.

From the strip thus made, cut two strips 57.5 cm (21½ in) long and two strips 61.5 cm (24½ in) long. Sew them to the Hourglass border.

For the fourth border (Flying Geese)

1   From the fabric chosen for the geese, cut sixteen 11.5 cm (4¼ in) squares. Cut each square twice, diagonally, to make sixty four triangles.
2   From the background fabric, cut sixty-four 6.5 cm (2³/8 in) squares. Cut each square into two triangles.
3   From the large floral fabric, cut four 9.5 cm (3½ in) squares.
4   Chain-piece one small triangle to one large triangle (Fig. 9). Repeat on the other side (Fig. 10). Make sixty-four Flying Geese.
5   Join them together in four rows of fifteen geese (sixteen if you are working in imperial measurements) (Fig. 11).

6   Sew a large floral square to each end of two rows of geese.
7   Sew the short rows to the quilt top, then the rows with the squares.

For the fifth border
From your chosen fabric, cut two 6.5 cm (2½ in) wide strips, each 87.5 cm (35½ in) long, and two 6.5 cm (2½ in) wide strips, each 77.5 cm (30½ in) long. Attach them to the quilt top.

For the sixth border (Four-patch)

1   From the background fabric, cut twelve 15.5 cm (6¼ in) squares. Cut the squares twice, diagonally, to yield forty-eight triangles. Cut eight 8.5 cm (3³/8 in) squares. Cut them once, diagonally, to yield sixteen triangles.
2   From two other fabrics, cut four 5.75 cm (2¼ in) wide strips, across the width of the fabric.
3   Sew one strip of each fabric together, making four pairs. Cut them into 5.75 cm (2¼ in) sections (Fig. 12).
4   Sew two sections together to make Four-patch blocks, giving a total of twenty-eight blocks (Fig. 13).
5   Sew small background triangles to two sides of the Four-patch blocks to make eight C units (Fig. 14).
6   Sew one large background triangle to the C units to make four D units (Fig. 15).
7   Sew one large triangle to the remaining C units to make four E units (Fig. 16).
8   Sew the remaining large triangles to the Four-patch blocks to make twenty F units (Fig. 17). Sew five D units together. Make four rows. Sew one C unit to the top of each row. Sew one D unit to the bottom of each row (Fig. 18).
9   Attach one row to the top and bottom of the quilt top.
10 Use two different colours for the cornerstones. From the first colour, cut four 10 cm (4 in) squares. From the second colour, cut eight 8.5 cm (3³/8 in) squares, then cut them once, diagonally,

Below: Detail of the centre star

to yield sixteen triangles. Sew a small triangle to each side of the square. Sew a cornerstone to each end of the remaining borders, then attach them to the quilt top.

For the seventh border

From the large floral fabric, cut two 22.5 cm (9 in) wide strips, 109.5 cm (45 1/2 in) long. Cut two 22.5 cm (9 in) wide strips, 151.5 cm (62 1/2 in) long. Attach the shorter strips, then the longer strips to the quilt top.

For the eighth border (Saw-tooth)

1   From two different fabrics cut five 7.5 cm (2 7/8 in) strips, across the width of the fabric. Cut the strips into fifty-nine squares (sixty-four if you are working in imperial measurements). Cut each square into two triangles.

2   Pair different fabric triangles and make 118 (128 if you are working in imperial measurements) Saw-tooth squares. Make two rows of thirty squares (thirty-three if you are working in imperial measurements) and two rows of twenty-eight (thirty-one if you are working in imperial measurements). Pin the two short rows

to the top and bottom of the quilt, matching centres and ends. Stitch. Pin and sew the side borders the same way.

TO FINISH

1   Cut the backing fabric in half across the width and remove the selvages. Join the pieces together along the long side.

2   Lay the backing face down on a large work surface. Centre the wadding on top, approximately 8 cm (3 in) from the edges. Trim any excess backing and smooth out any wrinkles. Place the quilt top on top of the wadding, face upwards, and smooth again. Pin and baste the layers together.

3   This quilt was machine-quilted in the ditch and professionally stipple-quilted in the seventh border. Begin machine-quilting in the centre Star block and work outwards. Not all the seams need to be quilted.

4   From the fabric set aside for the binding, cut seven 5.5 cm (2 1/2 in) wide straight strips across the width. Join the strips with diagonal seams. Bind the quilt, following the general instructions for binding on pages 13–14.

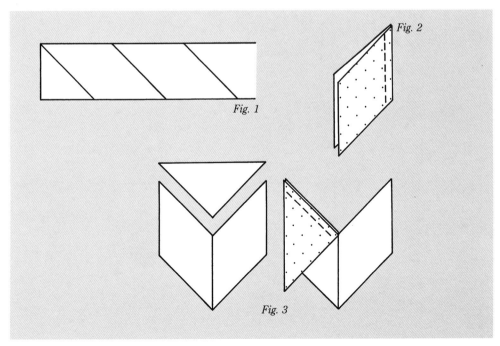

Fig. 1

Fig. 2

Fig. 3

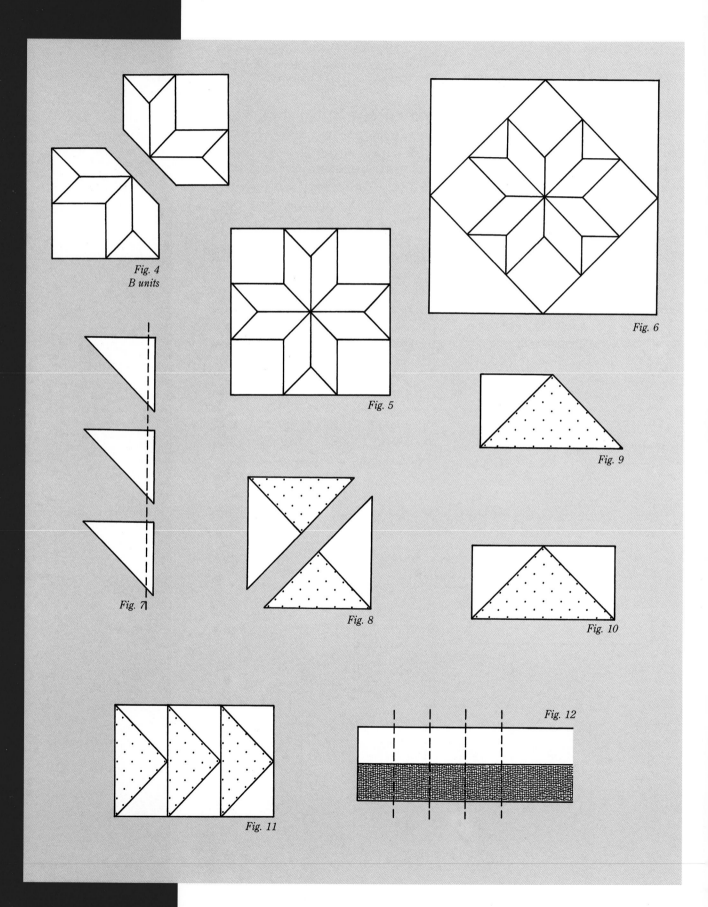

Fig. 4
B units

Fig. 5

Fig. 6

Fig. 7

Fig. 8

Fig. 9

Fig. 10

Fig. 11

Fig. 12

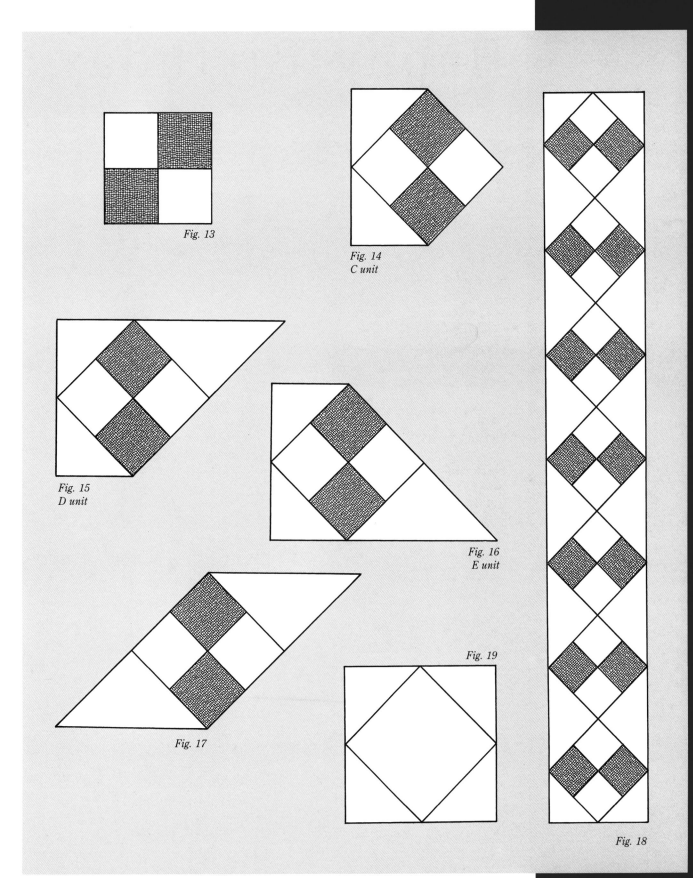

Fig. 13

Fig. 14
C unit

Fig. 15
D unit

Fig. 16
E unit

Fig. 17

Fig. 19

Fig. 18

Happy Birthday

YOU WILL NEED

For each block

- 7.5 cm x 50 cm (2⅝ in x 20 in) of dark fabric (A)
- 13.5 cm (5¼ in) square of light or medium fabric (B)
- 7.5 cm (2⅝ in) square of plain fabric for the centre (D)
- 2 m (2¼ yd) of fabric for the lattice strips
- 1 m (1⅛ yd) of fabric for the borders (E) (this includes fabric for the binding)
- 50 cm (20 in) of fabric for the side and corner triangles (C)
- 3 m (3¼ yd) of fabric for the backing
- 145 cm x 180 cm (58 in x 72 in) of medium- or low-loft wadding
- sewing machine
- 100% cotton thread
- rotary cutter and mat
- large and small quilter's rulers
- quilting hoop
- quilting thread
- quilting needles
- water-soluble marker pen
- usual sewing supplies

Signature, or autograph, blocks became very popular in the mid-1800s. Family and friends would sign or embroider a plain centre square for a block. The finished quilt would be presented to a person or family to mark a special occasion, generally the departure for a new home on the other side of the country, which often meant that there was only a small chance of the givers and receivers ever seeing each other again. As a consequence, these quilts were of great emotional significance. I have made this quilt as a record of birthdays of my family members, starting with my parents. I add the latest members of the family as they arrive!

Machine-pieced, hand-quilted
Finished size: 143 cm x 178 cm (56½ in x 70 in)
Block size: 18 cm (7 in)

CUTTING

1 From the dark strip (A), cut four 7.5 cm x 12.5 cm (2⅞ in x 5 in) rectangles
2 From the medium fabric (B) cut the square twice, diagonally, to yield four triangles.

From the side and corner triangle fabric (C)

1 Cut four 29.5 cm (11¼ in) squares, then cut them twice, diagonally, to yield sixteen triangles. Fourteen of these are for the side triangles.
2 Cut two 15.5 cm (5⅞ in) squares, then cut them once, diagonally, to yield four corner triangles.

From the lattice fabric

From the length of the fabric, cut eleven 6.5 cm (2½ in) wide strips. Cut four of these strips into forty 16.5 cm x 9.5 cm (2½ in x 7½ in) rectangles.

CONSTRUCTION

1 Sew two matching dark rectangles to opposite sides of the centre plain square (Fig. 1).
2 Sew the short side of a medium triangle to the opposite long sides of the remaining two rectangles (Fig. 2).
3 Assemble these sections into a block (Fig. 3). The rectangles may be too long; make the block square by placing a ruler over the block, aligning the side with the long sides of the triangles, and cutting the ends off the rectangles. Trim off the waste edges at the corners. Make as many blocks as you require. My quilt has thirty-six blocks.

ASSEMBLING

Sew the blocks, strips of lattice and side triangles into rows. Join the rows with long lattice strips as shown in the construction diagram on page 61.

For the borders

1 From the border fabric cut six 9 cm (3½ in) wide strips across the width of the fabric. Join all the strips together.
2 Measure the width of the quilt top and cut off two strips this length. Matching the centre of the border to the centre of the quilt top, and then matching the ends, pin and stitch the borders to the top and bottom of the quilt top.
3 Measure the length of the quilt, including the attached borders. Cut, pin and sew the side borders in the same way as the top and bottom borders.

HAPPY BIRTHDAY

QUICK TIP
For my nephew's twenty-first birthday, I made a quilt and had everyone attending sign it. There are many occasions that lend themselves to a quilt like this. Not only are they receiving your work of art, but also a memento of all those attending the occasion.

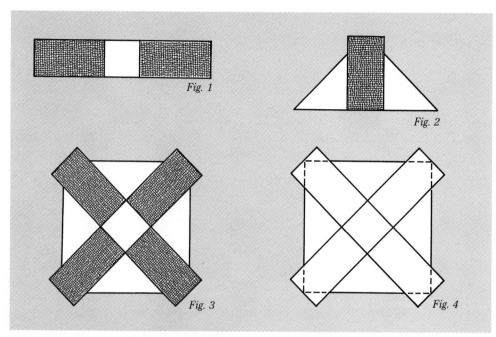

Fig. 1

Fig. 2

Fig. 3

Fig. 4

Above: Detail of one block

TO FINISH

1 Cut the backing fabric in half across the width and remove the selvages. Join the two pieces along one long side. Lay the backing, face down, on a large work surface. Centre the wadding on the backing and smooth out any wrinkles. Place the quilt top on the wadding, face upwards, and smooth again. Pin and baste the layers together.

2 I hand-quilted 7.5 mm ($^1/4$ in) from the seams in all the light areas. The borders were hand-quilted in a traditional cable design. Mark the quilting pattern as you go and remove all the pen marks when you have finished quilting for the day.

3 From the remaining border fabric, cut four straight 5.5 cm ($2^1/4$ in) wide strips for the binding or cut and join bias strips, if you prefer. Attach the binding, following the general instructions on pages 13–14.

Construction Diagram

Lollies

YOU WILL NEED

- one hundred and twenty-seven 11.5 cm (4½ in) squares of scrap fabrics
- 1.5 m (1⅔ yd) of fabric for the background
- 2.5 m (2¼ yd) of fabric for the backing
- 150 cm x 140 cm (60 in x 55 in) of medium- or low-loft wadding
- sewing machine
- walking foot (optional)
- 100% cotton thread
- rotary cutter and mat
- large and small quilter's rulers
- usual sewing supplies

Many years ago, I made a quilt similar to this, by hand over cardboard. I put it away half finished, when I was told the name of the block was 'Coffin'. Some time later, I read that the pattern was also called 'Lozenge', so I got it out and finished it! The method I use here is much quicker and easier than my original version, and very suitable for the new patchworker.

Beg, borrow or cut for yourself one hundred and twenty-seven 11.5 cm (4½ in) squares of your favourite colours and prints (this is the ideal quilt for using up squares from fabric clubs).

Machine-pieced, machine-quilted
Finished size: 150 cm x 137 cm (59 in x 54 in)

CUTTING
From the background fabric
1 Cut sixteen 6.5 cm (2½ in) wide strips. Cut them into 254 squares.
2 Cut six 17.5 cm (6¾ in) squares. Cut them twice, diagonally, to yield twenty-six side triangles.
3 Cut two 17 cm (6½ in) squares. Cut them once, diagonally, for the corner triangles.

From the border fabric
Cut six 10 cm (4 in) wide strips.

CONSTRUCTION
1 On all the small background squares, draw or fingerpress a diagonal line from one corner to another. With the right sides facing and matching the raw edges carefully, sew one background square to one corner of the large squares, sewing along the creased line (Fig. 1).

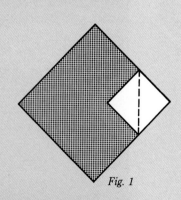

Fig. 1

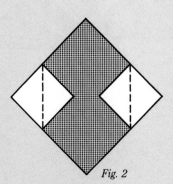

Fig. 2

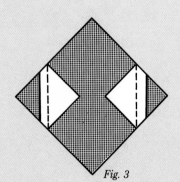

Fig. 3

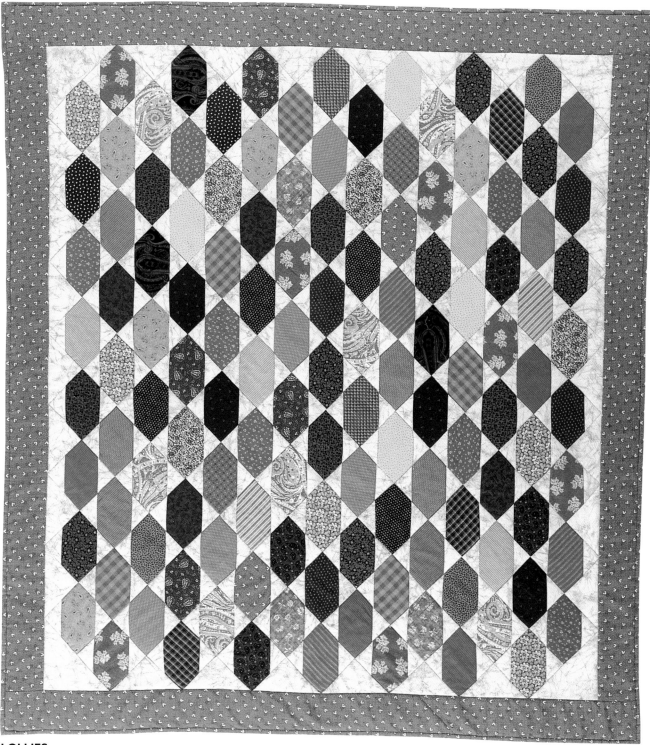

LOLLIES

Right: Detail of 'Lollies'

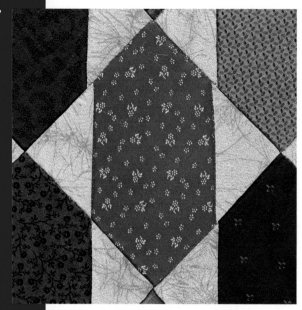

2 Sew another background square to the opposite corners of all the large squares, in the same way (Fig. 2).

3 Trim off the outer corners of all the small squares (Fig. 3) and press the remaining corner outwards to complete an A block (Fig. 4).

4 Sew four A blocks together to make a B block (Fig. 5). Make twenty-eight B blocks.

5 Using the A blocks and the side triangles, make five C blocks as shown (Fig. 6). Make one of figure 7.

6 Make six D blocks (Fig. 8). Make one of figure 9.

Construction Diagram

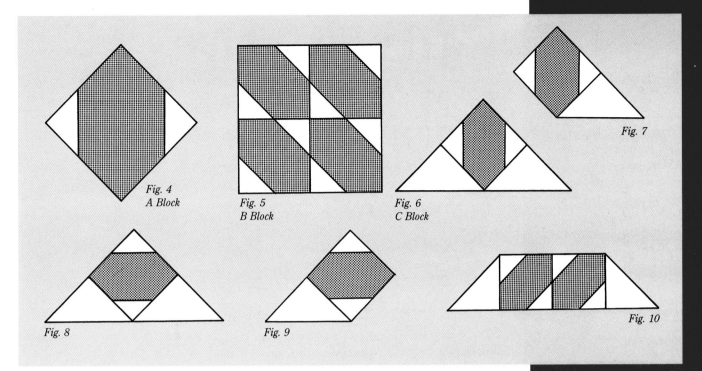

Fig. 4
A Block

Fig. 5
B Block

Fig. 6
C Block

Fig. 7

Fig. 8

Fig. 9

Fig. 10

7 Make one E block as shown (Fig.10).

8 Join all the blocks together in diagonal rows as shown in the construction diagram. Sew on the corner triangles last.

For the borders

1 Sew the six strips together to form one long strip.

2 Measure the width of the quilt top and cut two of the reserved border strips to this length. Pin the borders to the top and bottom of the quilt top, matching centres and ends. Stitch.

3 Measure the length of the quilt top, including the attached borders. Cut, pin and sew the side borders in the same way as the top and bottom borders.

TO FINISH

1 From the backing fabric, cut two 50 cm (20 in) wide strips across the width of the fabric. Join the pieces together along the short side. Cut this long strip to be 150 cm (60 in) long and sew it to the long side of the large piece.

2 Lay the backing face down on a large work surface. Centre the wadding on top, approximately 8 cm (3 in) from the edges. Trim any excess backing and smooth out any wrinkles. Place the quilt top on top of the wadding, face upwards, and smooth again. Pin the layers together.

3 I quilted in the ditch around the scrap pieces and the blocks.

4 From the fabric left over from the borders, cut ten 5.5 cm (2¹/2 in) wide bias strips for the binding. Join the strips with diagonal seams. Bind the quilt, following the general instructions for binding on pages 13–14.

QUICK TIP

If you are using precut packets of quilt squares and do not want to cut them down, you can calculate the small square size by halving the large square and adding one seam allowance. For example: if the large square is 12.5 cm (5 in), the small square would equal 6.25 cm (2¹/2 in) PLUS 7.5 mm (¹/4 in) or 7 cm square (2³/4 in).

Lady of the Lake

YOU WILL NEED

- 1.75 m (2 yd) of red print fabric (this includes fabric for the binding)
- 50 cm (20 in) of yellow print fabric
- 25 cm (10 in) of plain green fabric
- 20 cm (8 in) of navy paisley fabric
- good supply of light and dark fabric scraps equalling 1 m (1¹/8 yd) of each (some very small pieces can be used)
- 3.25 m (3¹/2 yd) of fabric for the backing
- 150 cm (60 in) square of wadding
- rotary cutter and mat
- large and small quilter's rulers
- quilting needles
- quilting thread
- sewing machine
- 100% cotton thread
- water-soluble marker pen
- usual sewing supplies

Placing this very traditional block on point, then turning alternate blocks once, gives this quilt a most unusual look. Using my 'old-looking' colours adds to the traditional look of this quilt.

Machine-pieced, hand-quilted
Finished size: 148 cm (58 in) square
Block size: 20 cm (8 in) square

CUTTING
From the red print fabric
1 From the length, cut four 16 cm (6¹/2 in) wide strips. Set these aside for the borders.
2 From the remainder, cut twelve 12.5 cm (4⁷/8 in) squares. Cut these once, diagonally, to yield twenty-four triangles.
3 Cut two 17.25 cm (6³/4 in) squares. Cut these twice, diagonally, to yield eight side triangles.

From the yellow print fabric
1 Cut twelve 12.5 cm (4⁷/8 in) squares. Cut them once, diagonally, to yield twenty-four triangles.

2 Cut two 17.25 cm (6³/4 in) squares. Cut them twice, diagonally, to yield eight side triangles.

From the green plain fabric
Cut thirty-two 7.5 cm (2⁷/8 in) squares. Cut them once, diagonally, to yield sixty-four triangles. Put sixteen of these triangles aside.

From the navy paisley fabric
Cut sixteen 7.5 cm (2⁷/8 in) squares. Cut them once, diagonally, to yield thirty-two triangles.

From the light scraps
Cut one hundred and ninety-two 7.5 cm (2⁷/8 in) squares. Cut them once, diagonally, to yield 384 triangles. Set sixteen of these triangles aside.

From the dark scraps
Cut one hundred and forty-four 7.5 cm (2⁷/8 in) squares. Cut them once, diagonally, to yield 288 triangles.

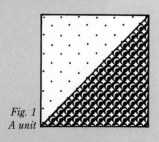

Fig. 1
A unit

Fig. 2
B unit

Right: Detail of 'Lady of the Lake'

LADY OF THE LAKE

QUICK TIP
For a modern effect, use jewel colours or geometric patterned fabrics.

CONSTRUCTION

1 Sew a 12.5 cm (4⁷/8 in) yellow print triangle to the matching red print triangle to make an A unit (Fig. 1). Repeat for all the triangles.
2 Sew the dark triangles (including the thirty-two navy paisley and forty-eight plain green triangles) to the light triangles to make 192 B units (Fig. 2).
3 Placing the navy paisley and the plain green triangles in the same position, sew the A units and B units together to complete the block (Fig. 3). Make twenty-four blocks.
4 Using the 17.25 cm (6³/4 in) red print and yellow print triangles, B units and the spare plain green and light triangles, make eight red side triangles and eight yellow side triangles (Fig. 4).

5 Sew the blocks and side triangles into diagonal rows as shown in the construction diagram.
6 Sew the rows together to complete the pieced top.

For the borders

1 Measure the width of the quilt top and cut two strips this length from the pieces already set aside. Matching the centre of the border to the centre of the quilt top, pin, then sew the borders to the top and bottom, following the general instructions for borders on page 11.
2 Measure the length, including the attached borders. Cut the side borders to this length. Pin, then sew the top and bottom borders in the same way as the side borders.

TO FINISH

1 Cut the backing fabric in half across the width and remove the selvages. Join the two pieces together along the long side. Lay the backing, face down, on a large work surface. Centre the wadding on top of the backing and smooth out any wrinkles. Place the quilt top on the wadding, face upwards, and smooth again. Pin and baste the layers together.
2 I hand-quilted 7.5 mm (¹/4 in) from the seams in all the light areas and quilted a knot pattern in the centre of the block and a braid in the borders, using commercial stencils. Mark your design as you go and remove all the pen lines when you finish quilting for the day.
3 From the remaining border fabric, cut twelve 5.5 cm (2¹/4 in) wide bias strips for the binding. Join the strips with diagonal seams to achieve the required length. Bind the quilt, following the general instructions on pages 13–14.

Above: Detail of four blocks

Fig. 3

Fig. 4

Construction Diagram

Scrap Sunburst

YOU WILL NEED

- ■ **3.5 m (4 yd) of plain green fabric**
- ■ **2.5 m (2³/4 yd) of plain cream fabric**
- ■ **good selection of fabric scraps, including florals, checks and small stripes**
- ■ **4.25 m (4³/4 yd) of fabric for the backing**
- ■ **200 cm (80 in) square of medium-loft wadding**
- ■ **50 cm (20 in) of fabric for the binding**
- ■ **sewing machine**
- ■ **100% cotton thread**
- ■ **rotary cutter and mat**
- ■ **large and small quilter's rulers**
- ■ **quilting hoop**
- ■ **quilting needles**
- ■ **quilting thread**
- ■ **water-soluble marker pen**
- ■ **usual sewing supplies**
- ■ **pencil**
- ■ **template plastic**
- ■ **compass**
- ■ **ruler**

I had much pleasure in making this quilt for my daughter Amelia, who chose all the fabrics. The end result is well worth the extra skill and care which this quilt requires. I would suggest new patchworkers make a practice block.

Many traditional quilts use variations on this design, which allows you to use up your stash of scraps.

Hand- or machine-pieced, hand-quilted
Finished size: 190 cm (76 in) square
Block size: 38 cm (15 in)

CUTTING

See the templates on page 74.
Trace the templates onto the template plastic and cut them out. The templates do not include seam allowances.

From the plain green fabric

1 From the length of the fabric, cut four strips, 14 cm (5 in) wide by 2 m (78 in) long.
2 From the remainder, cut nine 39.5 cm (15¹/2 in) squares.

From the plain cream fabric

1 Cut 144 of template A and 144 of template C, adding seam allowances.
2 Cut twenty-six 16 cm (6¹/4 in) squares. Cut them twice, diagonally, to yield 144 triangles.
3 Cut twenty-six 8 cm (3³/8 in) squares. Cut them once, diagonally, to yield fifty-two triangles.

From the scrap fabrics

1 Cut 144 of template B, adding seam allowances.
2 Cut three hundred and fifty-two 6 cm (2¹/4 in) squares.

CONSTRUCTION

1 Sew pieces A, B and C together into units as shown (Fig. I).
2 Sew sixteen of these units together to form a circle (Fig. 2).
3 Lightly crease the halfway and diagonal marks on the plain green squares. Open the compass to a 17.5 cm (7 in) radius and place the point in the centre where all the creases meet. Draw a circle. This is the sewing line. Close the compass by 7.5 mm (¹/4 in) and draw a second circle inside the first. This is the cutting line. Cut out the circle, beginning by carefully piercing the fabric with scissors along the cutting line.
4 On the remaining circle of fabric, open the compass to a 9 cm (3¹/2 in) radius and draw a circle. This will be the sewing line. Draw a second circle 7.5 mm (¹/4 in) larger than the first. This is the cutting line. Cut out this circle.
5 Matching the points of the diamonds to the crease lines of the centre circle, sew the pieced ring to the centre circle (Fig. 3).
6 Matching the points of the diamonds to the crease lines on the square with the circle cut-out, complete the block. Make nine blocks (Fig. 4).

ASSEMBLING
For the lattice strips

1 Sew the scrap squares to form eighty-eight Four-patch blocks (Fig. 5).
2 Using the large and small plain cream triangles and three of the Four-patch blocks, make twelve side lattice strips (Fig. 6).
3 Using the large and small plain cream triangles and thirteen Four-patch blocks, make four horizontal lattice strips.

SCRAP SUNBURST

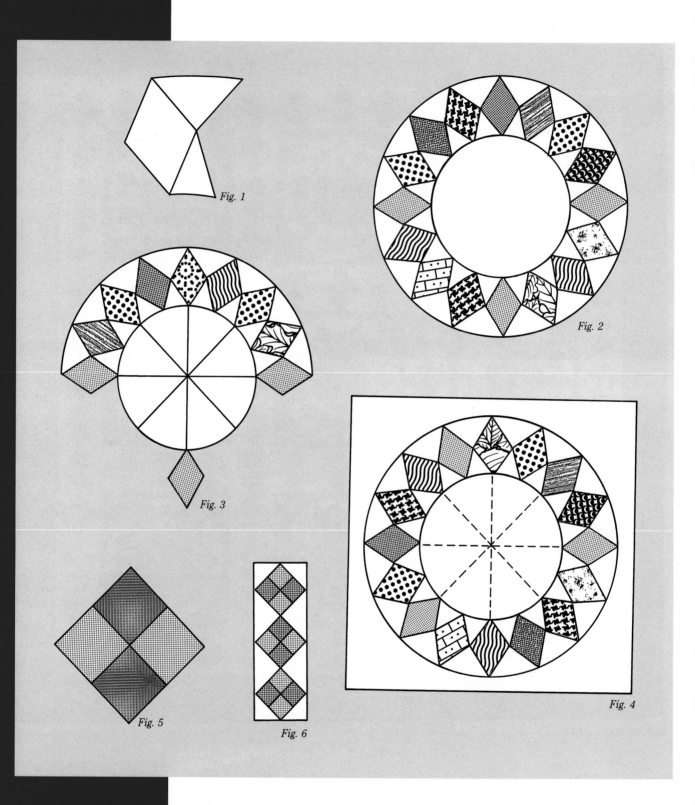

Fig. 1

Fig. 2

Fig. 3

Fig. 5

Fig. 6

Fig. 4

4 Assemble the blocks into three rows with a side lattice strip in between. Join the three rows with a horizontal lattice strip in between (Fig. 7).

For the borders

1 Measure the width of the quilt top and cut two of the 14 cm (5½ in) wide border strips to this length. Pin the borders to the top and bottom of the quilt top, matching the centres and the ends. Stitch.

2 Measure the length of the quilt top, including the attached borders. Cut, pin and sew the two remaining borders in the same way as the top and bottom borders.

TO FINISH

1 Cut the backing fabric in half across the width and remove the selvages. Join the pieces together along the long side. This seam will go across the quilt.

2 Lay the backing face down on a large work surface. Centre the wadding on top, approximately 8 cm (3 in) from the edges. Trim any excess backing and smooth out any wrinkles. Place the quilt top on top of the wadding, face upwards, and smooth again. Pin and baste the layers together.

3 I quilted 7.5 mm (¼ in) from the seams in all the white areas and used a commercial stencil for the blocks and the borders.

4 From the fabric set aside for the binding, cut eight 6 cm (2½ in) wide straight strips across the width of the fabric. Join the strips with diagonal seams as they are less noticeable than straight seams. Bind the quilt, following the general instructions for binding on pages 13–14.

QUICK TIP
Using a darker fabric at the corners, instead of the small cream triangles, will form stars at the corners of the blocks.

Fig. 7

TEMPLATES

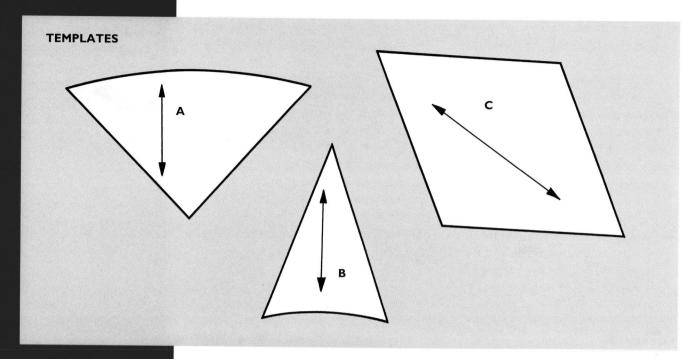

**Right: Detail of
'Scrap Sunburst'**

Windmills

Quilting is one of the oldest styles of needlework. Originally used for utilitarian purposes only, to hold three layers of cloth together, it soon became a way for quilters to show off their fine needlework skills. I have chosen this simple design because it provides large areas suitable for quilting. Whilst I enjoy the design aspect of quiltmaking, sometimes I just want to quilt. This quilt gave me that opportunity.

Machine-pieced, hand-quilted
Finished size: 204 cm (80 in) square
Block size: 30 cm (12 in)

CUTTING

From the ochre fabric

Cut twenty strips 7.5 cm (2$^7/_8$ in) wide across the width of the fabric. Cut these strips into two hundred and seventy-four 7.5 cm (2$^7/_8$ in) squares, then cut each square once, diagonally, to yield 548 triangles.

From the white fabric

1 Cut twenty strips, 7.5 cm (2$^7/_8$ in) wide. Cut these strips into two hundred and seventy-four 7.5 cm (2$^7/_8$ in) squares. Cut these squares once, diagonally, to yield 548 triangles.
2 Cut six strips, 11.5 cm (4$^1/_2$ in) wide. Cut these strips into fifty-two 11.5 cm (4$^1/_2$ in) squares.
3 Cut six strips, 6.5 cm (2$^1/_2$ in) wide. Set these strips aside for the first plain border.
4 From the length of the remaining white fabric, cut four strips, 11.5 cm (4$^1/_2$ in) wide. Set these aside for the third border.
5 Cut twelve 31.5 cm (12$^1/_2$ in) squares.

CONSTRUCTION

1 Sew all the ochre fabric triangles to all the white fabric triangles along the long side to make the A units. Make 548 A units (Fig. 1)
2 Sew 260 A units into 130 pairs as shown (Fig. 2).
3 Sew two pairs together as shown to make B units (Fig. 3). Make sixty-five B units.
4 Sew B units with a small white fabric square to make twenty-six C units (Fig. 4) and thirteen D units (Fig. 5).
5 Using two C units and one B unit complete the block (Fig. 6). Make thirteen pieced blocks.

ASSEMBLING

Join the pieced blocks and the large white squares into five rows as shown in the construction diagram.

YOU WILL NEED

- 5 m (5$^1/_2$ yd) of white fabric
- 2.5 m (2$^3/_4$ yd) of ochre fabric (this includes fabric for the binding)
- 4.5 m (5 yd) of fabric for the backing
- 205 cm (81 in) square of wadding
- usual sewing supplies
- quilting needles
- quilting thread
- quilting hoop
- water-soluble marker pen
- rotary cutter and mat
- large and small quilter's rulers
- sewing machine
- 100% cotton thread

Left: Detail of the quilting on 'Windmills'

QUICK TIP

To make the Windmill patch flatter, unpick the short seams back to the long seams, then push the seams in a clockwise fashion, as shown in figures 7 and 8.

For the borders

1 Attach the first white border as instructed in the section on mitred borders on page 11.
2 For the second border, make two rows of thirty-two A units. Sew them to the top and bottom of the quilt. Make two rows of thirty-four A units. Sew them to the sides of the quilt.
3 For the third border, attach it as instructed in the section on mitred borders on page 11.
4 For the fourth border, make two rows of thirty-eight A units. Sew them to the top and bottom of the quilt. Make two rows of forty A units. Sew them to the sides.

TO FINISH

1 Cut the backing fabric in half across the width and remove the selvages. Join the pieces together along the long side. This seam will go across the quilt.
2 Lay the backing fabric, face down on a large work surface. Centre the wadding on the backing and smooth out any wrinkles. Lay the quilt top on top of that, face upwards, and smooth again. Pin and baste the three layers together securely.

Fig. 1
A unit

Fig. 2

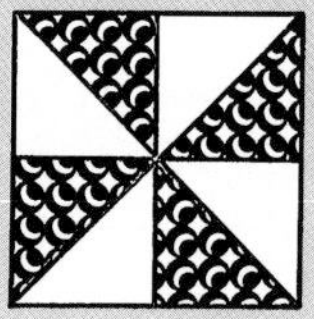

Fig. 3
B unit

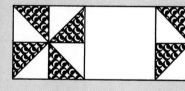

Fig. 4
C unit

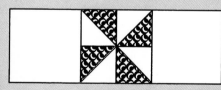

Fig. 5
D unit

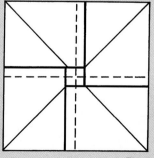

Fig. 6

unpick

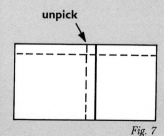

Fig. 7

Fig. 8

WINDMILLS

3 Hand-quilt in the design of your choice. I quilted diagonally in the Windmill blocks, quilted a feathered circle in the plain blocks and a fancy pattern in the borders. Mark your design as you go and remove any pen lines when you are finished quilting for the day.

4 Cut seven bias strips 5.5 cm (2¼ in) wide from the remaining ochre fabric for the binding. Join the strips with diagonal seams to achieve the length required. Bind the quilt, following the general instructions for binding on pages 13–14.

'Windmills' variation

Construction Diagram

**Left and Far Left:
Details of 'Windmills'**

Acknowledgments

I would like to thank the following people who helped me to produce this book: Traditional quilters for their inspiration; Ian, Belle and Amelia for their moral support and encouragement; Jan Ingall and Mary-Anne Miles for their help with the hand-quilting; Kerry Adams and Joanne Knott for their professional machine-quilting skills; Karen Fail and Judy Poulos for the opportunity; and my many students for teaching me so much.

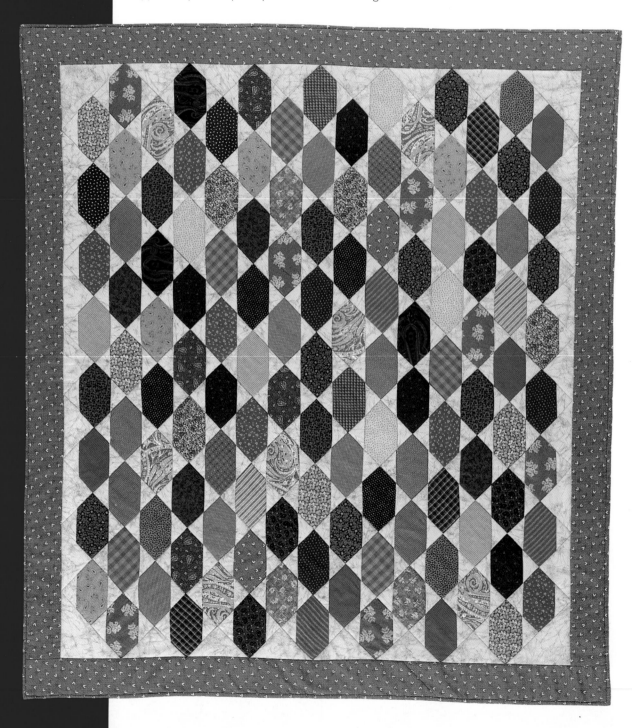